RESOURCES FOR NEW GROUPS

WOMAN'S SOCIETIES OF CHRISTIAN SERVICE
WESLEYAN SERVICE GUILDS

CREATION

out of

CHAOS

Woman's Division, Board of Missions, The Methodist Church

CONTENTS

TO DISCOVER	7
Who Am I? Who Are You? Who Are We?	8
United With Women Everywhere	19
The World Our Parish	32
Where the Atom Is Split	52
TO CREATE	70
Journey to Acceptance	71
For All Who Stumble	88
What It Feels Like to Be a Negro In White America	101
TO PARTICIPATE	115
In Dialogue With Women of Southeast Asia	116
TO ENCOUNTER	131
In Shared Sorrow	132
In Moments of Joy	148
TO INVEST	162
Ludhiana Made the Difference	163
Conversations in Poverty	177
Opportunity to Study	190
Focus on World Health—The Church And the United Nations	206
ORGANIZED FOR ACTION	220
Metamorphosis of a Circle	220
Diary of a Group That Wouldn't Fit a Pattern	224
The Giver and the Receiver	232
A Brief Historical Sketch of the Woman's Society of Christian Service and the Wesleyan Service Guild	235
Additional Resources	240
Evaluation Sheet	247

Foreword

This book came into being as a result of urgent and persistent requests for materials especially geared to the needs of new groups.

The title CREATION OUT OF CHAOS was chosen to help you understand and accept the various stages that people —whether as individuals or in groups—must experience before a sense of identity is discovered, a direction found, and a purpose formed.

A clue to the creative process is found in the story of Creation in Genesis:

"In the beginning God created the heaven and the earth. And the earth was without form, and void, and darkness was upon the face of the deep. And the spirit of God moved upon the face of the waters" (Genesis 1:1-2, King James Version).

From the Genesis poets we learn that before any new order can come into being, there is the chaotic. But remember that within the void and the darkness—the chaos—is the potential of form—creation. The chaos has to be embraced, literally accepted with love, before the new form can emerge. No one likes to risk chaos. We all cling to the familiar. To risk change is to risk failure.

This book is designed to provide help as your group goes through the various stages toward a healthy existence capable of making a strong contribution to your church, community and the wider world.

The creative group is characterized by the fact that it can live with the anxiety of change, temporary rootlessness and disorientation. Do not be afraid to experiment with new forms of programs, adventure into unusual projects, seek out people never before involved in church groups.

The fourteen programs provided here were developed

around the ideas in the membership cultivation leaflet—
You Are Invited to Join Women Around the World. They
suggest ways that your group can experience the dimensions promised in the "invitation to join." They offer a wide variety of subject matter and form.

We hope they will stimulate your group to formulate programs of your own, perhaps using them as examples of the kinds you can have. One actually was developed from a program put together by a local group. "The Metamorphosis of a Circle" is given so that you can get a glimpse at their growing concern for full participation and for acceptance of responsibility.

"The Diary of a Group That Wouldn't Fit a Pattern" is included to help you keep trying even when the purpose and destiny of the group are uncertain.

"The Giver and the Receiver" is not presented as a program but is included to point up the ambivalence in all we do. Remember that no matter how sincere your group is, you must not expect perfection. The day for romanticizing mission is over. Participating in church group activities is not an escape, but a participation in the realities of a broken world.

"A Short Historical Sketch of the Woman's Society of Christian Service and Wesleyan Service Guild" will help you get perspective as you seek ways of serving the present generation.

The "Additional Resources" list is very important. The audio-visuals, books of organizational structure, materials giving further information about the involvement of The Methodist Church around the world, and additional worship resources should be ordered as your group takes shape.

The "Evaluation Sheet," returned to the editor, will help in planning future materials.

Going back to the clue for creation in Genesis we are reminded that it was *God* who created—"And the spirit of God moved upon the face of the waters." The most that we can do is to cooperate with him in the act of creation out of chaos. This little book is to guide you in your cooperative act. All who have worked with the editor on it have been moved by the reality of this "spirit on the face of the waters," and we are confident that the words within these covers will be channels of this spirit, bringing creation out of chaos.

Hilda Lee Dail

HILDA LEE DAIL
Editor, Program Materials

to Discover...

your own identity
in moments of
involvement with
other women in
a cause beyond
yourself

Who Am I?
Who Are You?
Who Are We?

BARBARA CHAPIN

PURPOSE: To discover one another on a deep level.

PRE-PROGRAM PLANNING:

This is planned for a group which includes newcomers. If you allow it to be fun, many things can "happen."

Although a form is suggested, it is important to keep only the framework and to be extremely flexible about how it develops. The form has these purposes: to encourage every person to take part, if not in one question, then in the next by always coming around to each person and allowing choice for or against participation; it gives the leader a chance to limit the contribution of any one person. If someone monopolizes the time, or conversation moves into areas which seem too personal to be spontaneously revealed, the leader can simply call "time," even in the middle of a sentence. It is a good idea, especially if you don't know the group well, to warn them in the beginning that you intend to do this.

Groups should be assigned arbitrarily. There should be eight to twelve people in each. The easiest way is to number off (1, 2, 3, etc.) and then to go to group one, two, and three. This keeps people from staying with those they already know.

If all goes well, this program should help people open up to one another and to themselves on questions which are often thought but not articulated. Let us hope that it will lead to new inner explorations and to increased openness in sharing feelings and concerns.

Reading: EXODUS 3:13, 14, 15

Then Moses said to God, "If I come to the people of Israel and say to them, 'The God of your fathers has sent me to you,' and they ask me, 'What is his name?' what shall I say to them?"

God said to Moses, "I AM WHO I AM." And he said, "Say this to the people of Israel, 'I AM has sent me to you.'"

TO DISCOVER

God also said to Moses, "Say this to the people of Israel, 'The LORD, the God of your fathers, the God of Abraham, the God of Isaac, and the God of Jacob, has sent me to you': this is my name for ever, and this I am to be remembered throughout all generations." (From the **Revised Standard Version** of the Bible, copyrighted 1946 and 1952.)

LEADER:

Nearly everyone wonders at some time who someone else is, and then, "Who am I myself?" Often it is easier to get acquainted with others than with ourselves. Do we know who we are? Do we know people who are different from us? Do we *really* know very many people?

Today, we are mostly going to ask ourselves questions. In this kind of adventure, silence has its place. If you do not know what you think or feel, don't be afraid to stop and ponder. It is good to take time to consider in stillness.

What parts of our daily lives help us to understand each other and ourselves better? What activities help to expand our understanding? These are the questions we are going to explore today.

(Now the groups should split up, with one leader for each group. Put them in separate rooms if possible, or in areas enough apart that no one will be bothered by laughter or many voices. If seating is arranged in an informal circle, it gives a friendlier atmosphere, permitting everyone to see who is speaking. Call on people, one after another, in an established way, encouraging shy ones to join in, and inviting everyone to share. If the discussion becomes very deep in one area, linger there for awhile, but never exhaust the subject. Move on while there is still more to be said. Don't feel rigid about getting every question asked. However, keep the discussion from moving too far afield. Hold questions that are way off the topic for future explorations. At the end of an hour, no matter where you are in the program, call a halt, evaluate, and stop. The discussion will probably have been intense, and an hour is enough at one time.

In leading the discussion, have a minimum of notes so that you are always free to look at all participants and to be aware and sensitive to small signs that one or another would like to speak.)

I. LEADER: Let's get acquainted, and also explore how it feels to be moved about, whether by choice or of necessity. How is the feeling different or the same for people who travel or move into better neighborhoods, for refugees, migrants, fugitives, etc? (Read the questions and then turn to each person separately for the answers.)

Q. Who are you? Where were you born? Say quickly something your childhood home meant to you. (You may be surprised to find how many people who know one another well do not know where a friend was born, went to school, or had early roots.)

Q. How many in this group live in the same place they were born? In what countries are people apt to move often? What kind of people move? (Consider Africa, Asia, South America as examples.)

Q. Is mobility unique in our North American culture? What relation does it have to our Judeo-Christian tradition? What are some of the reasons why people move?

Q. What percentage of the U.S. population moves once every year? Every five years?

Q. Do you think we are basically a restless people? Why? Can you generalize in this way?*

Q. What has moving, or not moving, meant to you in your own life?

---
* See STATISTICAL ABSTRACT of the United States, U.S. Dept. of Commerce, Bureau of Census (available any library). See also THESE CITIES GLORIOUS, L. H. Janssen, Friendship Press, 1963.

II. LEADER: Here we may get into the meaning of identity, and how we hold on to our sense of our own individuality.

Q. When do you shake hands with a person you meet? Under what circumstances do you or do you not actually touch another person?

Q. How many people do you know by name? Who are the people you know by name whom you do not consider close personal friends? What name (first, last) do you use with that person? How do people address you? In what situations do you or do you not want to be called by name? When would you rather not have your name known? Why?

Q. Now let's pretend we don't know anything about one another, and I'll ask each of you to give me some identification by number as you do for a charge account or for renting a car. What is your social security number, your driver's license? What zone do you live in?

Q. Do you like this? Why? Why not? What feeling does it give you? How is it different from being asked for your name? Does something happen inside you when you think of yourself and others as numbers? Explain.

Q. Have you ever known someone who had a number from a concentration camp tattooed on an arm or leg? Or someone who has been in prison? Have you ever asked a person who has had this experience how he or she feels about numbers?

Q. Could you deliberately hurt a person whom you were looking at, and whose name you knew? Would it be harder than hurting someone you don't see or know at all?

Q. Under what circumstances do you prefer *not* to look at someone? How would you act when scolding a child? Refusing to give to a beggar? Explaining why you can't do something? When would you prefer to use a telephone instead of talking to someone face to face? Why?

III. LEADER: What we believe says a lot about who we are. The Methodist Church has a strong peace testimony. When a young man who is a conscientious objector refuses to join the armed forces, he has, in the past, been expected to do so in the grounds of his belief in a "Supreme Being." Those who object on non-religious, ethical, or moral grounds often are not willing to identify the force which compels them to act in this way. Now there is a Supreme Court ruling (Seeger vs. U.S.) making it possible to object without stating a belief in a Supreme Being.

Q. Why do people try to put a name such as "Supreme Being" on something they believe? Does it make the belief any more valid to call it by a specific name?

Q. Did God ever give himself a name, or means of identification? What was it? How do we think God indicated this to man?

Q. When you read about other faiths and cultures, do these experiences seem familiar or strange? Does it matter whether they are called by the same names? Can you understand what some of the unfamiliar customs and rituals mean even if they are done in completely different ways?

Q. What is the value of learning about different approaches to life, beliefs, and values?

IV. LEADER: How do we face making decisions between right and wrong as individuals? Many people try to "keep up with the Joneses." What judgment do *you* bring to bear on any situation or condition to decide your own actions?

Q. Suppose someone tells you to do something you think is wrong or harmful. Would you do it if the person telling you were your minister; boss; member of your family; good friend? What would you do?

Q. Suppose, for instance, your child has to take a course in school which you feel is harmful. What would

TO DISCOVER

you do? (If, for example, it is against your religious beliefs or would damage your child's natural creative ability.)

Q. Have you ever had to tell someone or a group *No* and mean it because you felt it was against your beliefs? How did you do it?

Q. Do you ever avoid getting involved in groups or activities because you are afraid you could not refuse if something were asked of you that you didn't feel you should do?

Q. When do you feel most yourself? When do you feel most real? Name some specific instance, if you wish, or be general.

V. LEADER: Lewis Mumford wrote some time ago:

"As our agents of destruction have reached cosmic dimensions, both our tangible fears and our neurotic apprehensions have increased until they are so terrifying to live with that they are involuntarily repressed. This repression is particularly notable in America, where it is marked by a virtual absence of any discussion or critical challenge of either our nuclear weapons or our ultimate aims. This is perhaps an indication of the unconscious guilt we feel for developing and actually using the atom bomb. Along with an unwillingness to face our own conduct or search for alternative courses, our behavior presents an even more dangerous symptom—an almost pathological sense of compulsion to pyramid our errors. . . ."*

Q. Do you think there are things we do as a nation or a group which are wrong, or afterwards prove to have been destructive? When that happens, what can we do as a group, or a nation, to make amends or say "We're sorry"?

---

* From "How War Began" by Lewis Mumford; reprinted with permission of *The Saturday Evening Post*, © 1959 The Curtis Publishing Company.

Q. Is there anyone you can think of—don't name out loud—in the community whom most people consider "wrong"? Any group, or any country? Is it because of their point of view, their way of acting, or some specific action?

Q. Do you think this person (or nation) is totally wrong? Do you think you had anything to do with the wrong you see? Do you think a day might come when he or she (or they) may seem very wise? Does what the person (or nation) is doing resemble anything you yourself do, or are tempted to do?

Q. Can you express what you feel about that person being wrong, and still love that person, and be open to the possibility that he or she (or they) may have something interesting and important to teach you after all?

VI. LEADER: In making decisions between right and wrong we often hurt others. Is this ever avoidable? How do you remember who you are when you are hurt? Or when you hurt someone else?

Q. Have you ever been in a spot where you did something you wished you hadn't, and then just couldn't find a way to explain, or make some kind of healing motion in the direction of someone you hurt? What happens to you in such a situation? What do you do to stop hurting inside?

Q. Take it the other way around: suppose someone hurts you? What kind of things happen inside you? What would happen if, as a result of someone else's actions, you found yourself in jail?

Q. If you had done something wrong and were sorry, but didn't know what to do, what could someone else do that would help you?

Q. Can you forgive yourself when you make a mistake? Can you forgive others?

Q. Does an "excuse" ever fit into the picture? Can it

ever be helpful? What is the difference between explaining why you did something wrong and making an excuse?

Q. What do courts, punishments, and jails do to people who have done something wrong or made a mistake? Do they give people a chance to see what they did wrong and try to change?

VII. LEADER: How can we change our thinking to include a new discovery, whether it's an idea, a belief, or another way of life?

Q. How many times in your life have you really changed course? Decided not to do something because it seemed wrong? Or the other way around: to do something which seemed very risky, but seemed right? Can you give an example?

Q. Do we need a Supreme Court ruling to help us turn and go in a new direction? Can we do it in our own lives without a law or outside directive?

Q. Is what you do wrong as important and as much a part of you as what you do right? Is anyone perfect?

Q. Is a mistake necessarily the end? Or is it a beginning? How can we make it so?

Martin Buber says we are always "becoming."

Q. Do you feel that you *are* always becoming—never complete, but always learning more, finding out more about yourself?

(Note to Leader: It is good to have a conclusion in hand in case the discussion does not come to something with a form to discover and bring out in summation. The following may be used in part or in whole. But far better if, in the course of the hour, enough has evolved for the leader to summarize and from it give a kind of direction for the future.)

Possible Conclusion

In a world of wonder, where no two snowflakes are ever the same, we should not be surprised to find that no two living creatures are ever the same, not that we can never completely understand one another. Nor should we be surprised to find that we do not like to be confused with someone else. Whatever we are, we like to be seen, appreciated, and accepted for that—not in comparison with some plastic mold which is set up as a criteria. Had creation wanted us all alike, we would have come that way. We didn't!

Therefore, let us remember this when we start to feel ourselves different from others. This differentness is our aliveness, and theirs. It is nothing to fear, and nothing to hide. To be unique is to be "you"—"me"—when we bring together what is unique in each of us we form a "we." Sometimes the unique "me" or "you" makes us do something that seems to go against society as a whole. Then we have to question. Is society really at fault? Is it trying to take from us what is really our own being? Or are we trying to impose what we are on others? Are we, perhaps, going against life? This is when we have to really know ourselves, and ask ourselves some hard questions about who we are, and why we act, or want to act as we do.

Being human, we are going to make mistakes. Let us, then, help each other to recognize our mistakes and to change, to learn, and to grow. When it is society which is making a mistake, give us the courage to support one another in standing against what we feel is wrong and in requesting change.

When we see people who seem to us to be doing something wrong, let us ask *why*? Perhaps we seem equally mistaken to them. Let us call each other by name, speaking to each other about what we feel is rich and full of joy and meaning. Let us share the humiliations of our mistakes and the warmth of healing.

Let us ask for a blessing with faith that, asking, we will be answered by name.

Reading—Genesis 32:26-30 (KJV).

And he said, Let me go, for the day breaketh. And he said, I will not let thee go, except thou bless me.

And he said unto him, What is thy name? And he said, Jacob.

And he said, Thy name shall be called no more Jacob, but Israel: for as a prince hast thou power with God and with men, and hast prevailed.

And Jacob asked him, and said, Tell me, I pray thee, thy name. And he said, Wherefore is it that thou dost ask after my name? And he blessed him there.

And Jacob called the name of the place Peniel: for I have seen God face to face, and my life is preserved. (Note to Leader: Some may feel it too "corny," but really it is a joyous ending to take hands, right and left, as in a square dance, and shake hands for a minute—even singing while holding hands.)

RESOURCES

"How War Began," by Lewis Mumford from the **Saturday Evening Post**, April 18, 1959. Also in **Adventures of the Mind**, by the editors of **Saturday Evening Post**, Vintage paperback, 33 West 60 Street, New York, N.Y. $1.65.

Patterns of Renewal, by Laurens Van der Post, Pendle Hill, Pamphlet Number 121, Wallingford, Penna. 45¢; 3 copies, $1.25.

The Phantasies of a Prisoner, by Lowell Naeve, Alan Swallow, Publishers, 2679 York Street, Denver, Colo. Paperback, $2.50.

Protest, by Elsa Bailey, American Friends Service Committee, 160 North 15 Street, Philadelphia, Penna. 19102. 50 cents.

I and Thou, by Martin Buber, Scribner paperback, 597 Fifth Avenue, New York, N.Y. 10017. $1.25.

ORDER THE FOLLOWING FROM THE SERVICE CENTER
7820 READING ROAD, CINCINNATI, OHIO 45237

Self-Study on the Meaning and Basis of Membership. For use in membership self-studies in local Woman's Societies and Guilds. 5 cents each; 6 for 25 cents.

You are Invited to Join Women Around the World. Leaflet for membership cultivation among women in the church who do not belong to the Woman's Society or Guild. Free.

ORDER THE FOLLOWING FROM THE WRIGHT STUDIO
5624 BROOKVILLE ROAD, INDIANAPOLIS, INDIANA 46219

(N.B. on orders less than $4.00, please add 25 cents for handling.)

Christian Witness Puzzlemat. Gaily colored rebus placemat suggests need of Christians to bear witness to their faith and to reach out to others. 20 for 75 cents.

World Neighbor Dolls. Cardboard cutouts of people from around the world, each in his own native costume and in color. Set of 12 dolls, $1.50.

ABOUT THE AUTHOR

Barbara Mather Chapin, born in Cleveland, Ohio, now lives in New York's Greenwich Village and is an editorial designer and an educator. She works free-lance in writing and designing, and is employed regularly as Consultant on Peace Literature for the American Friends Service Committee in Philadelphia, Pennsylvania. She also has worked as editorial assistant on the Committee on World Literacy and Christian Literature and was executive secretary, collaborator, and founding trustee of Artmobile, Inc.

She is a "firm believer in lay leadership in all fields," and she feels that "one great hope" of humanity is the development of "participatory democracy"—that is, the kind of action which is found in the freedom movement, in peace and freedom action, and in non-violent action, "which brings east and west together in a most hopeful meeting."

Although she loves the country and the sea, she lives in New York City, "perhaps because here is where you can get something like a total picture of our uniquely current challenges."

Among other interests are the American Association of University Women, the American Institute of Graphic Arts, the National Committee on Art Education, and the League of Women Voters.

United With Women Everywhere

VIRGINIA LAW

PURPOSE: To discover your own identity by understanding the bonds of mother-love, pride, concern, or sorrow which cross national and cultural boundaries, and through understanding to come to a realization of our unity.

PRE-PROGRAM PLANNING:

This program has been written for a leader and three readers. The leader's comments set the scene. You may wish to dramatize the individual scenes; perhaps each reader may want to read her part as a story—or you may think of some other way to make this material come alive for your group.

Let action grow out of the questions for discussion at the end of the program.

LEADER:

Riding home on a bus, two women sat discussing a third. She did everything so strangely. They simply couldn't understand how her children survived on the diet that she fed them. They couldn't imagine why her husband came home at all the way she kept house. And she dressed so queerly. The two went on and on comparing their ways of doing things with the ways of the other woman. Finally their conversation ended when one shrugged her shoulders in despair and said, "Well, we just don't have anything in common."

A missionary home on furlough from India had a phone call. "I hate to bother you," a voice said, "but I have a terrible problem, and I think you could help me."

"I'd be glad to if I can," the missionary said.

"You see," the woman said, "my daughter invited an Indian graduate student home with her from college. She

TO DISCOVER

accepted, and now my Susie has been elected to attend an important conference on international relations. Susie wants me to go ahead and entertain the Indian guest. I'd love to, but I wouldn't know what to *do* with her. We just don't have anything in common."

A Woman's Society officer at a Jurisdictional Conference stood with a registration form in her hand. She read, "Indicate if you will be willing to accept any roommate assigned you."

"This year all our conference will be integrated," she thought. "There will be delegates from the Central Jurisdiction. They might assign one of them as my roommate."

She remembered all her zeal for civil rights, her interest in voter registration, her concern for social justice.

"I'd like to accept just any roommate they assigned me, but we just wouldn't have anything in common."

A Negro student stood reading over the list of "Job Opportunities for Social Workers." Just three more weeks and she would be graduating. "Outstanding opportunity for qualified worker," she read, and then carefully noted all the attractions of this job, mostly family life service. She liked that. It certainly sounded good until she read, "Apply to: Mexican Migrant Mission."

She turned away disappointed. "I'd like that job IF I just had anything in common with Mexican migrant women."

On and on it goes, over and over again. A shrug of the shoulder, a sigh of regret, a look of disappointment, all voicing the lament, "We just don't have anything in common." We do it everyday with our own fellow Americans. What about those women from other countries? Naturally, we wouldn't have anything in common with them.

But we do. Women everywhere have the same basic needs for food, shelter, clothing, and protection. Women build their lives around fulfillment of these needs. Women bear their children, and in many places they are the food supply until their babies reach two years of age. Most women are the keepers of their home, the preparers of the food, and the protectors of the young. The old adage, "The hand that rocks the cradle, rules the world," is no less true in Africa, or India, or Japan than it is in America. Women are united around the world in more ways than we think.

Come with us now to the heart of Africa. Through the eyes of a missionary let us visit three Congolese women.

FIRST READER:

"Come here," a missionary friend called to me. "Look at this adorable Pygmy baby."

I walked over to where they stood under the shade of a palm tree. We were seven long days walk from any road. It was necessary to come that far to see the Pygmies, these forest dwellers who live in very temporary banana leaf huts and move about from one elephant kill to another. Even from this most inland village we still had to send a messenger telling the Pygmies we had arrived with medicines and nurses. This mother had come with her baby.

"Isn't this the cutest, tiniest baby you ever saw," my friend said.

"I don't think it's as large as Margaret's doll." Then, taking my tape measure, we measured it. "Just fourteen inches."

"These little fingers hardly look an inch long," the missionary said while holding them in her large white hand.

Lying there in her mother's arms, this human doll stretched and nestled closer, warming her bare body against the warm breast of her mother. The least fret and into her mouth went the nipple full of warm milk. Keeping dry was no problem. The mother simply held the baby out away from her body at some secret signal they had. No wet diapers bothered them. This baby had no clothing, no brightly colored rattler, no sweet-smelling baby oil; but she was the picture of perfect contentment as she nestled there, warm and snug in her mother's arms.

The mother was just forty-six inches tall. Only by looking at her face could I begin to guess her age. She looked hardly large enough for a fifth grade child. Her hands were rough and calloused from hard digging in the forest for roots to fill her family's empty stomachs. There were white spots where hot steam had left its burning mark. Scars now healed traced the path of some sharp knife, leaving forever a witness of toil, sacrifice, and suffering for a woman who tried to rear a family in a Pygmy village.

Standing near this mother were two other children, about two years apart in age. Each had been nursed at her breast until it began to walk. As the next pregnancy came, the toddler moved on to eat out of the family pot, and expectations began for the new baby. Leaning close to their mother, these children looked like life-sized dolls. Their heads were covered with bloody spots where the nurse had shaved away the hair to get the white man's itch medicine next to the infection. Tears stained their faces, and their eyes looked with distrust upon me; they pressed closer to their mother. She reached down and patted each of them. "It's all right," she reassured them; and looking up at her, their fear vanished and trust filled their eyes.

Looking at this Pygmy mother, I recalled the image of my own mother. She was a schoolteacher. Often she played the piano while we sang, read stories when we were washed and ready for bed, knelt beside us when we said our prayers, checked to see that our teeth were brushed or that we drank our milk, first out of "air proof" bottles and later out of glasses. This Pgymy mother would never be able to give any of these things to her children.

But were these the things for which I remembered my

TO DISCOVER

mother? No. What I remembered best was lying awake in the dark, cold night listening to some strange sound, my heart in my throat, straining to breath silently; then mother would open the door and come into my room. "Mother, what's that noise?" I asked. "That's just the wind blowing in the trees," she would say. Then, kissing me on the forehead and tucking me in tighter, she would add, "Everything's all right; you go to sleep." With that assurance I would turn over and go to sleep. As a child, I no more understood why this was so than the little Pygmy child understood why his fear vanished, but the reasons were the same.

SECOND READER:

Going into a remote village in Congo to be the first white woman could always be an interesting experience.

With my husband and me often went our five-year-old daughter, Margaret Ann, a little towhead with straight hair pulled to one side and held fast by a bright colored barrette.

One afternoon we drove up and stopped in a very remote village. Seeing us, someone shouted, "Mama Leeeee," and clapping her hands together rushed over to greet us. Down the street we could see other villagers stopping their work and looking toward the car. Then our greeter shouted louder, "My people! A white Mama has come with a white child."

This word was magic. Dropping whatever they were doing the people came rushing and crowded around us.

"Ahhh, Dikambu dia mambo (marvelous feet)," they said.

"Look at her hair," one said.

"It's white," another marveled.

"Wonder what they put on it to turn it white?"

"Is it a boy or girl?"

"Boy," one answered.

"No," answered another, "it's a girl."

"Mama, is it a boy or girl?"
"It's a girl," I said.
"What's her name?"
"In English or Otetela?" I asked.
"In Otetela."
"Amena (beautiful one)."
"Truly, she is well-named. What's it in English?" someone asked.
"Margaret Ann."
"What does that mean?"
"It doesn't have a meaning. It's just a name," I said.
"Listen, the white man gives his child a name with no meaning." They marveled at such strange ways.
"What's your child's name?" I asked one near to me.
Pointing to one child the mother said, "Ona Koko." Translating this I knew the name meant, "Child of a chicken." She pointed to others, " 'From a goat,' 'heavens,' 'lightning.' "
"What strange names with meaning this mother gives to her children," I thought.
Most of the children wore nothing at all, or else one small dirty rag hanging draped from a string about their low loins. Their little pot-bellied, worm-filled stomachs hung out over the string belt. Their navels were protruding, ruptured by the weight of the worms and the half-cooked rice they gorged on at one big meal a day.
"When did this baby walk?" I asked.
"Five months ago," the mother answered.
I knew she had weaned him then. The babies were fat and roly-poly, but by the time they were two years old they looked lean and gaunt.
"What does he eat now?" I asked.
"Just like we do," she answered.
This meant that the young child was either eating rice and cassava leaves hot with pepper, or he wasn't eating, and I could guess which it was.
"Does he eat well?"

TO DISCOVER

"Not yet," the mother said, with the resignation of one waiting for this to take place. Hanging from a nearby bush was a stalk of lovely, ripe bananas.

"Does he like bananas?"

"Oh no! He hasn't eaten bananas yet; they'd give him worms."

I stood thinking about this. When I first heard that although ripe bananas were falling off the trees wasting, the land was filled with hungry two year olds, I was irritated at such ignorance. Then Margaret Ann came into our family and became our prize banana eater. Returning one afternoon from a woman's meeting I found my husband, Burleigh, amused. "I don't make too good a baby sitter," he said. "I thought Margaret Ann had worms."

"Why so?" I asked.

"When I washed out her soiled diaper, I noticed many small objects about one-inch long." Then he chuckled, "On close inspection they turned out to be banana fibers."

I could understand, but how could you expect an illiterate Congolese mother with no possible idea of food fibers, yet fully aware of stomach worms, ever to understand this.

Pointing to Margaret Ann I said, "She ate bananas every day when she was that age. She doesn't have worms."

"Truly?" she marveled.

"In my country bananas don't grow like they do here in Congo. They come from far away. We pay more for just one kilo than you do for a whole stalk. Our doctors tell us that bananas are one of the best foods you can find for babies. So, though they are so very expensive, mothers still buy them. Our babies love to eat them."

A murmur rose from among the women standing listening. One asked, "Your doctor tells you to feed them to your baby?"

"Yes." Again they discussed this fact. They had

25

TO DISCOVER

heard of the mission doctor. They knew of the miracles he performed, the babies he had saved.

Pointing to the Congolese male nurse traveling with us I said, "You ask him about feeding bananas to your baby. He can also tell you how to cook cassava leaves so your baby will eat them right now. You must be careful. Your baby needs food."

It would have done no good to explain to her that in Africa over fifty per cent of all the babies die before they are three years of age. The most dangerous time is when they are weaned. Babies literally starve to death until they can learn to eat adult foods. Neither would it have helped to tell her that in my country we are distressed if the infant mortality rate increases even by one per cent. It hurt me just to think of the difference.

How simple it seemed to explain that if she would only cook the cassava leaves without the hot pepper, the baby would eat it. To give a spoon full of very hot food to a young child just off the breast would cook its mouth. No wonder the child didn't like it. Naturally the mother knew adults loved this hot, hot food, but it is hard for her to imagine someone not liking the food she likes best. I would just have to leave all this for the nurse to explain. They knew that he, too, liked the hot, peppered cassava leaves. He could explain better than I why such food is not best for babies and young children.

But I must remember that a low infant mortality rate was not always so in America. Until we began to teach about child care, we filled our cemeteries with small, three-foot-long graves. There is always so much to be taught. I knew many things just because those among whom I had grown up knew them. I had learned many more things in school and college. Others had worked to discover this knowledge, write the books, and then teach me. Certainly my life has been blessed by knowing this. Now I must pass on this knowledge with its blessings.

THIRD READER:

I had been in charge of the Woman's School at the Wembo Nyama Station, the oldest and largest Methodist Station in Central Congo. Hygiene was one of the many subjects we were to teach. Most of the students had babies. Every afternoon the 2:00 o'clock bell rang, and we could see them coming toward the school, each with her baby strapped to her back. Sometimes they carried a toddler on one hip. Toddlers could be left in our nursery, but the nursing baby had to stay with its mother. No *good* mother would ever get farther than the length of one breast from her baby. A church baby fold would be a shocking arrangement to these mothers.

It seemed to me that a good beginning for my hygiene class would be "How to Bathe a Baby." From this point we could study baby care, then child care, and on to adult hygiene. I gathered up all the supplies I needed: baby's bathtub, soap, cloth, towels, even the baby, for my Margaret Ann was only four months old at the time.

My water carrier brought two big buckets of warm water. We placed a table under the shade of a palm tree, and my lesson began. With detailed explanations of why and how, I proceeded to bathe my model. She kicked the water and squirmed about, but we got her clean and laid her out on the table to dry. Then my teacher's instinct told me that I hadn't gotten through to my class. Looking about, I could see my demonstration had amused more than it had informed these women. Something was wrong.

I cleared away the display, dismissed the class, and went home discouraged, all the while turning over in my mind the experiment and evaluating it. Leaving Margaret Ann with a nurse, I rode my bike down to the village. Mama Shimba lived in our mission village. She was the wife of a nurse and had been to school through the fifth grade. She had two little boys just about the ages of my two sons. In fact, the four played together almost everyday. When they came to play in my yard, I had often

TO DISCOVER

remarked how clean and spotless they were. I knew she had other children in the two-year spacing plan, and that not too long before, a new baby had come who was only a few months older than Margaret Ann.

When I rode into her yard she was sitting out behind the house in the shade of the overhanging eaves. I took the chair offered me, and we sat visiting. Finally I got around to the reason for my visit. "Would you show me how you bathe your baby?"

Taking a large clean woven grass mat, Mama Shimba laid it out in the sun. Right in the middle she placed her naked little girl just sitting up. Taking one cup of warm water she began to let this slowly trickle down the baby's head. Moving around from side to side, these trickles of water completely wet the baby's body long before even that one cup was empty. Then, taking the bar of soap —no washcloth—she worked up a white lather. Reaching out she took a few grains of sand and worked this into the lather on the little girl's hands and between her toes. "Here the children get itch so easily," she said.

At our home we used a cute yellow fingernail brush, but the sand served the same purpose and was much more available. Mama Shimba began to trickle another cup of water down over her baby, washing away the dirt and soap. It was amazing how clean one cup left her. Lifting the baby, she moved her to a clean spot on the mat and another rinse began. Then, completely clean of soap, the baby was placed on a second mat to dry in the warm sunlight.

Riding home, I marveled at this perfect demonstration. Little wonder that the students had found me more amusing than enlightening! I wouldn't bathe my baby in a bathtub either if I had to walk a good mile to the spring and bring all the bath water in a bucket on my head. Just the same, Mama Shimba's baby lay in the sunlight as clean as my Margaret, even without a bathtub, washcloth or towel. I knew that the next afternoon when Mama Shimba taught the lesson on bathing a baby, the students would learn something.

LEADER:

Women everywhere face the same problems in rearing their families: food, clothing, and shelter (even if only in a limited degree). Many are limited by the resources available. We sometimes forget this, surrounded as we are by overabundance. All women are motivated by the same basic concern of mother love and self-preservation.

Looking back at the women we have just met, let us consider our own involvement as well as theirs:

—Why did the three women feel that they had "nothing in common" with:

The guest from India?
The Negro roommate?
The Mexican migrant?

—And what factors of education, language, difference, culture, etc., often make us feel "different" from others—or that they are very "different" from us?

—What are some of the ways in which these six women do have something in common? With one another? With us?

—Is the love of a Pygmy or Congolese or American mother different? How? Why? If they are the same, discuss how they are.

—Do you think that Pygmy children experience more mother-love because they are always so close to their mothers than do American children who are frequently separated by time spent in school and in watching television? Why or why not?

—In what ways would you liken the Pygmy mother's reactions toward having medical aid to those of a person in this country going to a welfare clinic? Would the reactions be similar? How or why not?

—Did you, your mother, or your grandmother eat beef at six months of age? Drink fruit juice before a year old?

Eat bananas as a baby? Consider some eating or health habit you have had to change since you were a child.

—Why was Mama Shimba's method of "bathing the baby" much more effective than the missionary's? List some of the advantages of Mama Shimba's method.

—How would you try to get to know someone with whom you feel you have "nothing in common?" Are there such people in your community? In your church? How can you discover what you do have in common?

"Love is patient; love is kind and envies no one. Love is never boastful, nor conceited, nor rude, never selfish, not quick to take offense. Love keeps no score of wrongs; does not gloat over other men's sins, but delights in the truth. There is nothing love cannot face; there is no limit to its faith, its hope, and its endurance."*

RESOURCES

Missionary Itineration:

For information about how to get a missionary to speak at your church, and for much other information related to his visit, see the excellent little pamphlet **Your Church and the Missionary Visitor.** Order free from the Service Center (except for postage and handling in quantities: 20 copies, 25¢; 50 copies, 45¢; 100 copies, 65¢.)

For a "Speakers List" of names and addresses of missionaries on furlough (or retired, or nationals on leave), write to your Conference Secretary of Missionary Education and Service. ("Speakers List" issued Jan., May, Sept. List of Conference Secretaries can be found in the Directory of the Woman's Division; order from Service Center. 50¢.)

ORDER THE FOLLOWING FROM THE SERVICE CENTER
7820 READING ROAD, CINCINNATI, OHIO 45237

Picture Packets. Sets of six 8 x 10-inch black and white glossy photos with caption sheet, title cards and suggestions for display

---

* (I Corinthians 13:4-7. From *The New English Bible, New Testament.* © The Delegates of the Oxford University Press and The Syndics of the Cambridge University Press 1961. Reprinted by permission.)

for the following areas and concerns: (Each $1.50) Africa, India, Medical Missions, Pakistan.

What Can We Do? By Ruth D. See. Practical handbook on race relations. 75¢

Leaflet in the "Methodist Work in New Nations" series: **Democratic Republic of the Congo.** Free.

Music from the New Nations. (Available from Service Center and Cokesbury.) A 12-inch 33⅓ rpm record of folk music, patriotic music, and Christian hymns demonstrating the cultural and spiritual vitality of new nations in Africa and Asia. Explanatory notes on jacket. (BOM) Sale only $5.00.

ORDER THE FOLLOWING FROM THE WRIGHT STUDIO
5264 BROOKVILLE ROAD, INDIANAPOLIS, INDIANA 46219

Africa Proverbs Napkin. Paper napkin in fresh green and brown illustrates the proverbs and activities of the women of Africa. 50 for 80¢.

ABOUT THE AUTHOR

Mrs. Burleigh Law and her husband, an industrial arts missionary, served in Congo fifteen years, first at Wembo Nyama, the oldest Methodist mission station in Congo, and later at Lomela where they pioneered in opening up new mission work—a school, churches, and medical services in the outvillages of the Batetela Tribe.

Mr. Law was killed August 4, 1964, in Wembo Nyama by rebel soldiers after flying in to rescue five other missionary families.

Mrs. Law grew up in Chipley, Florida and attended Asbury College, Wilmore, Kentucky, where she met her husband. Later she was graduated from Florida State University; and recently she began graduate work on an M.A. in Christian Education at Scarritt College, Nashville, Tennessee. She and her children, David, 21, Paul, 19, and Margaret Ann, 12, now make their home in Nashville. Mrs. Law is the author of **Assignment Congo**, a book about their experiences, published in 1966 by Rand McNally. It can be ordered from the Service Center or from Cokesbury.

Protestants; they are minority among the largely Mormon population.

We got here early last evening, picked up our rental car at the airport, and then checked in at a motel for the night. You know us: we got an early start, and it was a beautiful drive up through the evergreens. Then we drove between and over ridge after ridge of mountains until we came to Glenwood Springs. This is all winter and summer resort area, only about fifty miles from Aspen.

Methodist Deaconesses Ada Duhigg and Mildred May met us here. These two modern-day pioneers came here in the spring of 1964 with "Phoebe," their International Travelall and "covered wagon" (house trailer to you). They headquarter in Basalt, at the foot of the bridge where the Frying Pan and the Roaring Fork Rivers meet. Virtually the entire western slope of the Rockies, part of the Methodist Utah-Western District, is their parish. Sponsored by seven denominations (Baptist, Christian, Episcopal, Lutheran, Methodist, Presbyterian, United Church of Christ) they are the Utah Protestant Mobile Ministry.

Last night we met a group of young people who helped fix up the church in Thomasville, a tiny community twenty-two miles up the Frying Pan from Basalt. It was a lively and delightful evening. Besides the fun, they found time to discuss what they could do for the Mobile Ministry this summer and decided to help with an interdenominational vacation school.

I'm so glad we had this contact as this is proving to be a most exciting trip. Not only is it a grand vacation, but I think we might even learn something! The social work needs in an area such as this are unique, yet in so many ways similar to those to be met in the city. It only points up how basic are our human needs, wherever we are. Time for a coffee before we start out. Best to all.

Louise

LETTER #2   Denver, Colorado
                             en route to Manila
Dear Jane,

Here we are at the Denver airport waiting our flight to start us on the next leg of our world journey. But let me tell you some of our adventures of these past few days. Really, you've no idea how and where we've traveled since we left this airport just a little over a week ago.

We really intended to write while we were in Basalt, but there simply wasn't time. It was a perfectly beautiful trip to Basalt. We even saw deer along the highway, and the birds! How wonderful it is to hear birds singing after hearing only the noise of the city.

It was good to renew acquaintance with Ada and Mildred, and we had news of many friends to share. You'd be amazed at what these two are doing way up here on the western slope of the Rockies. The story of Thomasville will illustrate what they're doing as well as why.

Thomasville is a little community a good twenty-two miles up the river above Basalt. I shouldn't call it a "good" distance, since it's a rough, rugged road that winds along the river 'til you reach the tiny settlement. Because of the Ruedi Dam hundreds of construction workers are moving here from all over the country.

Some people missed the church. They felt the need for Christian education for their children as well as themselves. Well, during the summer of 1964 some of these men and women acquired an old one-room schoolhouse no longer in use, cleared away the cobwebs, dust, and dirt, and had a potluck supper by candlelight. From this beginning they started having Sunday afternoon church services and a church school.

In the fall a group of young people and their counselors from ten churches—the MYF subdistrict—made up a team to help fix up the place. They came with wire paint scrapers, paint, brushes, rollers, mops, buckets, soap, rags—the works. I can imagine they made a real caravan as they went up the winding road to Thomasville. Then they dug in and cleaned the little building inside and out. The Woman's Societies of four communities (from a radius of 30 miles) provided meals. One church gave pews, another loaned a pulpit, another sent along several gallons of paint, while another sent song books and plastic storm windows. Still another group had a cross cut out of the native red rock for the altar, and made available an old pump organ.

Within a matter of a few days what had been a rundown schoolhouse became a growing church. Talk about transformation! Ada showed us some pictures they took before all the work began, and you just wouldn't recognize the place. We drove up with Ada and Mildred for Sunday service and found a small but eager group awaiting us.

Ada and Mildred are a familiar sight along these mountain roads, and everyone knows "Phoebe" (the car) and the trailer. Working together with the various ministers, these two women help provide training for youth workers, Woman's Society leaders, study groups, Scouts, weekday church schools; they often fill in as speakers, conduct preaching services, baptisms, and funerals. This is not an easy job, especially in winter. Yet Ada and Mildred spin off the miles going from place to place ministering to the needs of these folks who are seeking a closer fellowship with one another and with Christ. As I watched these two women working tirelessly, I was struck with a sense of awe at what they are accomplishing.

Tomorrow we reach Manila. I'm sure it will be quite a change from Colorado! But I'm also sure we won't find anything much more challenging than what we've seen here. 'Bye for now; more later.

Mary

LETTER #3

Dear Ann—and greetings to all,

Manila, P. I.

We arrived in Manila yesterday and had a most delightful introduction to the islands by air. This is quite a contrast to the mountains of Colorado. The only similarity is trees and greenery, but this lush, tropical growth is altogether unlike the evergreens. Here the greenness penetrates the air so that everything takes on a hazy tone.

The people are friendly, and I'm reminded of Southern California with all these white, Spanish-style buildings. The biggest contrast is in the streets. Traffic is composed not only of cars, but bicycles, carts (some hand-drawn, some pulled by animals), rickshaws of various kinds, motorcycle taxis, and people. This is the BIG impression: People, people, and still more people!

We contacted Miss Madaleine Klepper, the director, at the Manila Methodist Center. We heard about the Center at the last Social Work Conference we attended. Madaleine, a Methodist missionary, began this work around 1950 after seeing the great need for some such program in this particular area.

I must say it certainly has all the elements of urgent need. The Center is located on a tremendous piece of land between two contrasting sections of the city. On one side are thousands of frame shacks built higgledy-piggledy, squeezed together, more than overflowing with people, children, chickens, and dogs. On the other side are some twelve blocks on which are located college and university buildings with a student population of more than two hundred thousand.

A huge playground—almost a square mile—seems to be in use all the time. The Center itself is a homey, rambling building that seems to expand once you have stepped inside.

There is a dormitory for college girls who cannot afford the housing provided by the educational institutions. Each year there is increased demand, but they accommodate only about two dozen girls, not all of them Christian, nor all of them Protestant.

Besides the college-university students, the Center is concerned about providing other educational programs.

There are three kindergartens. Those who can pay, do; and those who can't, don't. What they're trying to do for the high school dropouts is fascinating and way ahead of us at home. They recognize the need to motivate as well as educate. Out of fourteen youngsters in one of their first groups, twelve were re-enrolled in regular school before the year was out.

It was quite thrilling to see such an active and advanced program going. I must say it began to give me a new idea of missions. Guess I was a bit surprised to discover how much like home this was. I'll let Mary tell you about the next leg of our trip. It has developed a bit unexpectedly. Tomorrow we tour the island and then head for Bangkok, Rangoon, and India. 'Bye for now,

Louise

LETTER #4

Manila, P. I.

Hi there, Ann,

It hardly seems possible that we've already begun our "world tour." I have to pinch myself occasionally to be sure it's really true.

This experience is refreshing because of new sights and sounds, depressing because there's still so much that needs doing, and tremendously challenging.

We did agree before we left home that *this* trip was, primarily, to give us an educational experience in new phases of social work. But, naturally, we still want to see as much else as we can possibly squeeze in, and with Louise's penchant for organization we may manage to see more than I think. Our schedule is already knocked out, though, on our very first visit. Instead of spending only a morning at the Manila Methodist Center, we spent an entire day. As Louise has written, we were completely enthralled with their program and how it has developed.

Now I must tell you what is coming up the next leg of our trip. When we left home we still weren't sure about our contacts in India, nor just how much chance we'd have to see any projects of interest. Now we'll stop briefly at Bangkok and Rangoon—strictly for sightseeing—and then head for Calcutta and what we believe will be a unique adventure.

Remember when we were trying to track down unusual projects, and I wrote to the Methodist Board of Missions? Eventually we heard about this rather new project near Calcutta, and so we wrote directly to the folks in charge there.

Well, when we arrived at the hotel in Manila, there was a big, fat letter waiting for us, filled with details about the Ecumenical Social and Industrial Institute (ESII) and the project in Durgapur. They invited us to spend a whole week with them, and we just decided to accept.

Our contact is Miss Val Maynard Smith, a British missionary who has been associated with this program since the latter part of 1963. She's been loaned to the staff by the Anglicans (Church of England—Episcopal in the U.S.). Actually, the project had only just begun shortly before that when the Reverend Kenyon Wright, an English Methodist minister, was assigned to the area. About the same time, the government of India began to develop a tremendous industrial complex in the Demodar Valley northwest of Calcutta. It's now referred to as "The Ruhr of India."

Really, it's fantastic what is happening there. Read what Miss Smith wrote about the area in a booklet, "The Church in Durgapur":

"A traveller on the Grand Trunk Road from Calcutta to Delhi in the early months of 1956 might well have hoped, on reaching mile-post 110, to see a panther lurking in the jungle which bordered the road. Today, only seven years later, it is here that the Grand Trunk Road enters its ten mile course through the new city of Durgapur. The word 'city' is perhaps misleading, for Durgapur is, in fact, not one town but a number of different industrial concerns, each with its own 'township.'"

When we first read this we had to shake our heads. This certainly didn't sound like the India we had read about in travel folders or books. Granted, our reading hasn't been too broad, but to think of industry and a ten mile long city—well! This just wasn't the picture we had of India being 80 per cent villages with thatch and mud houses, poverty, disease, and struggling toward literacy. Naturally the prospect of seeing a "different India" appealed to us, and this sounds like a really new concept of the church at work in the community.

We can hardly wait to get there. Tomorrow we head for points west. Yes, west of here, although it seems like we should really say "east" since we've always thought of this as the "far" east . . . don't know why, though I suppose it once was "far," but today it most surely is right next door.

That's all for now. Off we go, and more later.

Mary

LETTER #5

Durgapur, India

Dear Jane,

Bangkok and Rangoon have been left behind—as well as a steamy night in Calcutta. Whew! What a night! One night in Calcutta comes about as close to a Turkish bath as I'd ever want. The streets were teeming (looked up some figures: Calcutta has more than seventy-five thousand people per square mile as compared to New York City, which has *only* twenty-five hundred)—crowds of people! People on foot, on bicycles, driving oxcarts, driving horsecarts, in motorcycle taxis (and boy! is there a scramble to keep out of the way of those), clanging streetcars with people clinging on the sides or sometimes on top. At night there seem to be literally millions, and I guess maybe that's not far wrong, walking the streets, sitting at little cubbyhole tea shops, and sleeping on the sidewalks. You actually have to pick your way around, over, and past bodies if you go out for an evening walk. We were told that these refugees are now raising the second generation who have known only the sidewalks of Calcutta for home; thousands of them live in meager shelters of reeds, thatch, cardboard, or sometimes tin that seldom stand alone, but lean against buildings, walls, or whatever they can find for support.

I felt depressed. Maybe it was just the oppressive weather, but there seemed to be so many people—too many—and seemingly so little being done for them. Oh, there are many agencies, and the government has built new housing. But, as it is in any slum or congested city, such measures seem like a mere drop in the bucket compared to the overwhelming need.

It was a relief when Miss Smith met us and we started out for Durgapur. At least now we're out of the hot, steaming caldron that is the Calcutta metropolitan area.

This is our first Indian train ride and, to say the least, it's quite an adventure! It reminds me of a state fair, rush hour travel, and a camping trip all rolled into one—that is, if you can imagine such a combination!

Miss Smith is a most delightful person, and quite British. She's had a wealth of background for this work, we discovered when she took us out for a bit of sightseeing the night we were in the city. During the war she served with the women's branch of the British Army, and spent two and a half years in Egypt. Then she was the company secretary for a large firm of building and public works contractors. For seven years, (she really doesn't look old enough, but she insists she has worked all these years), she had the sole pastoral charge of two parishes in Sheffield where her parishioners were steel mill workers and coal miners.

She called for us early in the morning and we left, all three jammed into a motorcycle taxi. We sat packed into two facing seats with our baggage in our laps and piled between. It's probably a good thing the baggage was there for it prevented our seeing too much of the oncoming traffic. Dodging sacred cows—yes, they even roam the streets of the city—and herds of goats, other taxis, trucks, streetcars, we learned something about "immovable objects and irresistible forces!"

To get to the rail station we had to go across the Howrah Bridge which crosses the Hooghly River. Howrah is still a part of the main Calcutta metropolitan area, but it's on the mainland where the train is. We could only catch glimpses of the river itself as we dashed across, along with what seemed like a million others. If you look at a map, you'll see that this whole area is just river delta—fingers of land laid down over the centuries by the endless flow of waters from the north. The Ganges is so sacred that to drink of these waters is thought to be especially meritorious for one. There are always clusters of animals and people bathing, washing clothes, or dipping bucketfuls for drinking and other purposes. In addition, there are strings of wooden barges, tugboats, and ocean freighters lining the river banks, or anchored in midstream.

We arrived at the station without mishap. Railroad trains and stations in India are quite different from those in the U.S. Most trains are the European style. Each car is sectioned into compartments which are fitted out in first to third class (the first being the best). In first class are springs or padded couch seats, but in the third class are only narrow wooden benches. Some compartments are designed for women only, but people usually travel all together; and if you're in third class this could even include sharing the compartment with a goat! If you go any great distance, you must take everything with you from bedding to food and water. Thus, the station platforms always look like the beginning of an encampment with piles of people, tin trunks, bedding, water jugs, food baskets, and maybe a few dogs. It always seems that the women, the children, and the dogs are piled with the baggage while the men wander about importantly. When the trains pull in, it's a mad scramble to get aboard. They are on the level with the platforms, but it's not an easy thing to get into a compartment, even if you have a reservation, without being swept off your feet in the rush. Then as the train pulls out—after you're squeezed into the small compartment space—half the people jump off and you discover they were only seeing someone off.

It's quite an experience, and we can now chalk up another travel adventure. The trip from Calcutta was filled with new sights, sounds, and smells! More later, if we're not completely exhausted.

Yours truly,
Louise

LETTER #6

Durgapur, India

Dear Betty,

I don't know where to begin—and I can hardly stop. Everything has been so new and exciting.

The scenery on the way to Durgapur was delightfully green and constantly changing. Around Calcutta it was quite congested with buildings, houses—multiple-story apartments—and various industries. Then we came into the valley where it was suddenly rural: fields of wheat, yellow mustard, and sugarcane. Next were cool, inviting groves of mango trees with the fruit just getting ripe. At our first station we bought some, and how good they were!

However, it only seemed a few more miles 'til the scenery changed again, and quite suddenly we were seeing bare earth, stark, new steel buildings, and massive sheds of huge industrial complexes. Quite abruptly we're out of "typical" India into a new land entirely. The industrial revolution has forged steel mills out of mango groves and dug coal mines beneath wheat fields. For ten miles the rail line and the Grand Trunk Road run between mills, mines, machine industry, and rows and rows of new housing. This is Durgapur!

TO DISCOVER

We arrived last Monday, and it's now Thursday night. There's just so much to see and do that we're extending our stay so we can be here over Sunday. We both agreed that we wanted to take part in a Sunday service at the church in Durgapur (a united church—Methodist, Baptist, and Anglican).

It's really hard to sort out, from all the many experiences we've been having, a *few* to write home about. There are several pamphlets which tell about the Ecumenical Social and Industrial Institute (ESII). We're sending you a packet. It seems that the whole object of this team ministry in Durgapur is to develop "the kind of total ministry, and the forms of church life which will enable the laity to find Christ in the life of Durgapur, and thus enable Durgapur to see Christ." We read this in the "Plan of Joint Action" which continues: "Therefore the pastoral ministry and the industrial team are not separated—for we believe that industrial mission must not be something extra to the normal pastoral and worship life of the churches."

It's an entirely new concept of the church in the community. And isn't it strange that it has begun way out here in India! These ideas would be just as pertinent and practical in Chicago or Pittsburgh as in Calcutta and Durgapur. The facts about this development are not only in statistical reports, but right before our eyes in looming steel girders and buildings, in black, belching smoke stacks, and in dark, cavernous coal mines.

Right here is eighty per cent of all of India's heavy industry; four of her five steel works (including the largest); two of her major coal fields. And the growth has only just begun! It is reported that this rapid industrialization is likely to continue for the next twenty-five years. I tell you, it's more than a stretch of one's imagination to comprehend. Just try to picture what the industrial revolution of the Western world would have been like had it taken place in thirty years instead of about two hundred! There are people here who, only a few weeks or months ago, were driving an oxcart in a village; and today are building jet planes in a factory!

Here are a few more facts and figures to make your head swim. In less than ten years the population has grown from hundreds to hundreds of thousands. Most of the people live in the company-built housing projects. Those not employed by the companies do not qualify for such living quarters. They are pouring into the area and putting up shacks of all varieties. Eventually they propose to build from eighteen thousand to twenty thousand multiple-unit dwellings. Other community facilities built by the companies include hospitals, schools, health centers, shopping centers—about the only thing I haven't seen is a Western-style supermarket, but at the rate things are going, I can imagine a supermarket will open up any day.

The church began here almost from the start. They acquired land right in the middle of one of the townships and built in 1961. That was the Durgapur United Church. It has grown, and under the new plan will be one of several centers, each located in one of the townships. Together they will be known as *The Church in Durgapur*. Each individual church will have its own pastoral ministry, appointed in the usual way. But each of these pastors will also be a member of the industrial team ministry of Durgapur. They've already begun to build a staff of specialists (part of the team), which includes social welfare, youth work, industrial relations.

According to their Plan ". . . it must be stressed again that we do not expect these workers to do the job of industrial and social mission *for* the church, but rather to establish the Christian groups and cells in industry, society, etc., and train the lay leaders in these spheres, so that the *whole* church becomes aware of its responsibility for the whole of life." (The italics are theirs.)

It is thrilling to see this beginning to function. Still experimental, the team is trying to develop a pattern so they can really reach out into the community, drawing into the life of the church—not just the life of the church as expressed by Sunday church attendance, but the life which is expressed in everyday involvement with fellow workers.

The Reverend Kenyon Wright, director of the Institute, besides helping start the united church, was one of the first who helped initiate the idea of the Institute. He is English and a Methodist minister. Talking to him makes me reach back into the hazy corners of memory for history about John Wesley—for this all seems to be just a new application of his original concern for the working man: that Christ and his church was relevant to the man in the mines and the mills as well as to the man in the parliament and the pew.

This has certainly been an eye-opening experience for both of us. I only wish that we could initiate such a project at home. Maybe we'll have to ask the Indians to come to us as missionaries. There's a lot we could learn from them. This week has gone so fast. From here we return to Calcutta and then do a hop-skip-and-jump across North Africa, Europe, and back to New York. Maybe we'll have time somewhere along the line to sort out a few more impressions and reactions to all this.

'Bye now . . . more later.

Mary

LETTER #7

Durgapur, India

Dear Betty,

If you'd told me when I left Chicago that I'd spend a whole week practically roughing it in a raw industrial development on the fringes of steaming jungles—and enjoying it—well, I wouldn't have believed you.

As I sat on the edge of the bed last night and began to realize that it was our last in this place, I was suddenly surprised to find I got a bit of a lump in my throat. Honestly, there's something about this place, these people, and the tremendous challenge of this project that has gotten hold of me. If I were used to using such phrases, I'd almost say that maybe I'd been converted since I came here. For the first time I begin to see just what it can mean to "be the church in action."

We've gone into homes with Miss Smith and with Miss Mukerjee (the young Indian girl social worker), if you can call these crowded flats "homes." These families have left village homes to seek a new life in industry, just as our fathers moved from the farms of Iowa to the steel mills of Gary.

To the Indian, the family means a great deal. They've had the joint-family system for centuries. Suddenly it is coming apart at the seams, and here are the young people—couples, or new families—breaking off from the security of living within the walls of the family home. It's the same old story, but with a peculiar new element of pathos. Perhaps when those first farmers moved from Iowa they found flush toilets, sinks, and people living just the other side of the wall as strange and sometimes frightening as do these families coming from the villages of India. But I doubt it. What do you do when you can no longer have a man with a goat come to your door to deliver milk? What do you do when you don't know the man who sells you fruit and vegetables?

Add to this the language problem. More than twenty different ones spoken here. Some people know one or two, and, on occasion, they can speak to each other in Hindi, or perhaps even in English (of a sort). But often they can't really communicate with one another. It's worse than the Tower of Babel.

Social work was just a profession before; here it's begun to look like and mean more than a job. Why, I'd even go so far as to say that it could be a calling. Guess I've never known, or given much thought to how we may be called to express in our everyday contacts what we claim to believe on Sundays.

As we lay in this sticky heat last night, we couldn't go to sleep. But it wasn't entirely due to the weather. I'm not sure what's happened. Both of us are experiencing something we can't quite define. It's a feeling, but that doesn't explain it, really. I think I'm in the process of changing my whole outlook on life—even death. It has a different meaning here where the mortality rate is still tremendously high, and where the life span is just a bit over forty (which puts me practically in the patriarchal range!). Life and death seems to go together: on the heels of mourning is joy for a new life. You have no time to be morbid; life is new and vital. I think maybe this is the kind of real living that our pioneer forefathers felt as they moved out across the western plains. I'm beginning to realize what it was that Ada and Mildred had that made them seem like pioneers. I dug out my scrubby little paper dictionary and these words leaped at me: "PIONEER—to open a way in advance of the main body." And I suddenly began to realize that this is what we've been taught about Christ: he was not only opening a way, he was The Way. Certainly he was a pioneer, and so all those who are seeking to help others find a better way of life today must be pioneers. I'm not sure now if I'm a pioneer or a missionary. Can you imagine it? Me, a hardened caseworker, a missionary? Well, you just wait and see.

As ever,
Louise

LETTER #8

Calcutta, India

Dear Jane,

We're back in Calcutta just for one brief night. Tomorrow we leave for North Africa and Europe. We'll spend several days on the Mediterranean relaxing and also sorting out the varied experiences of this past week.

The Ecumenical Social and Industrial Institute is one of the most exciting programs I've ever seen. Seeing it, we've both experienced something we can't quite define.

It's far deeper than "cultural shock" and perhaps more meaningful and lasting than a so-called "mountaintop experience." These folks are finding something vital in their Christian living, and it's not going to stop even at the far-flung extremities of Durgapur.

The most exciting thing is that I've been offered a job here. Yes, the Ecumenical Social and Industrial Institute (ESII) is trying to build their team and they need more social workers. When I casually mentioned that this was my sabbatical year and that I planned to do some private research and study, they fairly jumped at me, asking if I might do that "research and study" here. What to do? It's most tempting. And it most certainly is a challenging situation.

But I'm not really sure I belong. After all, I'm not a missionary—or, on second thought, am I?

We got to discussing that the other night, Louise and I. You know her thinking on the subject. But we both had to agree that what we had seen here and in Manila wasn't what we'd thought of as "missionary work." At least it's not the old stereotype. Perhaps that's our mistake in thinking that it has to be a certain type and pattern.

Well, I'm seriously considering this. I could extend my sabbatical. The need is so great. At least I could be helpful in training some Indian social workers as they come onto the staff here.

Strange, we were both just commenting how "homesick" for Durgapur we felt already. I tell you, there's absolutely no telling where you will end up when you start out to discover what's going on around the world—especially what's going on in the church around the world. It's been a revelation to us to discover how much we have been able to contribute just in our short visits. At the same time we have gained tremendously. In these few weeks we've seen Methodists (both American and British) at work around the world. We've seen the church at work around the world and very much *in* the world. Certainly Ada and Mary are dealing with people in their life situations. Manila Community Center is reaching out to meet the needs of children, youth, and adults in their congested section of the city. And ESII is setting a new pattern for moving into the life and work of individuals to meet their needs, to help them meet the challenges of labor relations, and to help them find a way to witness in the coal mines and steel mills.

We spent more time here than we'd planned. But it's been worth every minute. It may be that we working women in the United States are missing a real area of service. There seem to be many places for short term help, and I think I'm ready to give a year. Guess it's the least I can do if I claim to be really concerned about the state the world is in just now.

Well, I'll get off my soap box and finish this. It's been wonderful. Wish you could all have been here to share it with us. But we'll try to bring some of it home.

> Our best, as always,
> Mary

RESOURCE MATERIAL

ORDER THE FOLLOWING FROM THE SERVICE CENTER
7820 READING ROAD, CINCINNATI, OHIO 45237

World Federation of Methodist Women Place Mats. The "Tree of Life" symbol and pictures of World Federation groups on a green and cream place mat. 12 for 75¢; 100 or more, $6.00 per hundred.

World Federation of Methodist Women Napkins. Imprinted with the "Tree of Life" symbol. 12 for 25¢; 100 or more, $1.50 per hundred.

World Federation of Methodist Women Post Card. May be used as a personal mailing card or as an attractive place card at banquets. (Available also in Spanish; when ordering please specify if Spanish card is wanted.) 5¢ each; 6 for 25¢.

Map—World Federation of Methodist Women. Beautiful colored map showing the units and areas of the World Federation and their interrelationships. $1.00.

Leaflet in the "Methodist Work in New Nations" series: **Republic of Philippines.** Free.

For free pamphlet listing seven 1966 mission tours, write to:
Department of Field Interpretation
Board of Missions of The Methodist Church
475 Riverside Drive,
New York, N.Y. 10027

ORDER THE FOLLOWING FROM THE WRIGHT STUDIO 5264 BROOKVILLE ROAD, INDIANAPOLIS, INDIANA 46219 (N.B. on orders less than $4.00, please add 25¢ for handling.)

Christian Witness Puzzlemat. Gaily colored rebus placemat suggests need of Christians to bear witness to their faith and to reach out to others. 20 for 75¢.

World Neighbor Dolls. Cardboard cutouts of people from around the world, each one in his own native costume and in color. Set of 12 dolls, $1.50.

For information about missionary personnel, recruitment, and itineration, see "Where the Atom Is Split, Let the Church Be United."

ABOUT THE AUTHOR

Miss Murden Woods is a native of California but spent most of her life in the Pacific Northwest where her father is a Methodist minister. She holds a bachelor of arts degree from the University of Puget Sound and a master of arts degree from Syracuse University. For several years she served in home mission and religious education in Texas, California and Oregon. Later, she was director of religious education of the Central United Protestant Church of Richland, Washington.

In 1949 she went to India as a short-term missionary (I-3) for the Woman's Division. After completing graduate work at Syracuse University, she was assigned to Lahore, West Pakistan, for work in adult literacy and the development of literature with The Methodist Church and the West Pakistan Christian Council.

At present she is under appointment with the Woman's Union Missionary Society to return to West Pakistan. While waiting for a visa, she has been working in the Asia Department, Division of Overseas Ministries of the National Council of Churches; the Joint Commission on Education and Cultivation; and for the Woman's Division.

Where the Atom Is Split, Let the Church Be United

MURDEN WOODS

PURPOSE: To discover through involvement in ecumenical endeavors how this can lead you across denominational, racial and national boundaries into a new understanding, both of yourself and of the "church universal."

PRE-PROGRAM PLANNING:

1. Have members of the group gather background information on:
    a. other "United Protestant" endeavors
    b. areas of Protestant unity in your community
    c. consider the importance of unified Protestant efforts overseas (Note relationships between the National Council of Churches in the U.S., National Councils overseas, and individual denominational boards and agencies.)

2. Have someone gather background on attitudes of scientists to religion.

PROGRAM PRESENTATION:

This is a play which can be presented very simply with only chairs and tables as properties—or as a regular drama. Chairs and tables can be used to simulate most staging. There are five parts, but four persons can read all the parts. (i.e. person reading **Ann's** part could also be **Prem**)

Since the life experience of **Martha** and **Nancy** provide the worshipful climax, be sure to capture this in any adaptation. Worship is not a time set apart, but those points in daily living when we suddenly are aware that "God is here."

TO DISCOVER

RESOURCES

Household of God—Lesslie Newbigin, Friendship Press, New York, paperback, 1953, $2.25.
The Pressure of Our Common Calling—W. A. Visser 't Hooft, Doubleday, 1959, $2.50.
One World, One Mission—W. Richey Hogg, Friendship Press, 1960, paperback $1.50; study guide, 50¢.

Consult or interview local officers of Council of Churches, Ministerial Association, or other cooperative, interdenominational groups.

Perhaps interview a Christian and a non-Christian scientist in your community.

"Where Religion and Science Meet"—Roland Gittelsohn, **Saturday Review**, March 23, 1963.

Check various publications in past few years for interviews with Astronauts Glenn, Grissom, Carpenter, etc.

ACTION GROWING OUT OF PROGRAM

1—Discover ways in which you can participate in interdenominational projects and programs in your community. (Check with United Church Women or your local Council of Churches)
2—Get acquainted with the missionary outreach of The Methodist Church through:
   The Prayer Calendar—order from Service Center
   World Outlook
   The Methodist Woman
3—Contact furloughed or retired missionaries in your area (See **Prayer Calendar** for addresses; also see page 239.
4—For information regarding interdenominational programs, write Division of Overseas Ministries of National Council of Churches of Christ in the USA, Office of Interpretation and Promotion, Room 630, 475 Riverside Drive, New York, New York 10027.

Scene I

(At stage left Martha Wesley is packing a trunk—use a large carton or place two chairs on their sides, seat to seat. She picks up a worn pamphlet from among piles of books, clothing, etc., stacked on the floor and thumbs through pages.)

MARTHA (*reads*): "Where the Atom Is Split, Let the Church Be United" . . . it seems ages since those words first aroused my curiosity. (*Sitting on the floor among piles of belongings.*)

MARTHA: Hmmm . . . what's this I wrote on the margin? Oh, yes, I remember . . . "Spare no effort to make fast with bonds of peace the unity which the Spirit gives" (Ephesians 4:3). That was Reverend Jim's text my first Sunday here in Richland. Goodness, what's happened to me these past four years. Here I am going overseas to serve the church as a missionary, to teach physics and maybe even do literacy work! What could have been further from my mind four years ago? It seems like only yesterday I arrived in Richland for the first time. (*She continues "packing" and reminiscing.*)

MARTHA: Doc Phillips brought me here. He said ever since I'd been his student back in college he'd wanted me to do research with him. He and Ann came here more than fifteen years ago. They sure knew a good man when they got one.

(*Knock or bell—Martha goes to side of stage and ushers Ann into room. Ann's arms are loaded with small parcels.*)

MARTHA: Hi there, Ann. You look like Santa Claus. (*Ann walks over to "trunk" and drops packages on floor.*) Don't tell me all those have to go in that trunk, too? On the phone you said "a few little things," but I should have known that you never mean "little-little" . . . it's always "big-little." (*They both sit on the floor.*) Do you realize it was just four years ago tomorrow that you and Doc and the folks from Central Church welcomed me to Richland? Remember that evening?

ANN (*laughing*): Do I remember! You can't say we gave you any chance to get lonesome although we hadn't really expected you to get so completely involved in church affairs that very first night. But Jim Cox is that kind of a minister. He believes that every member of his church can only discover what it means to be a part of the church if they're actively involved in it.

MARTHA: That's the truth! It was just like old times back home in Houston. You and Doc were always up to your ears in church activities there. I didn't expect you'd be any different here. (*Packs a few things—then says reflectively.*) Yes, Jim certainly believes that everyone has a mission, and it seems like most of his congregation agrees with him. Don't know how I could have been more actively involved, what with explosive fifth graders in my church school class and jet-propelled junior highs in Youth Fellowship. . . .

ANN (*interrupting*): To say nothing of some uninterested, unenthusiastic—until you arrived on the scene—church women.

MARTHA: Now, Ann. They weren't really uninterested. They just didn't know very much about the Wesleyan Service Guild. And even if we did have a hard pull to get going, the first five of us, especially, have come to a new understanding of our mission. You know it's been these experiences in teaching young people—as well as those literacy classes for migrants—and working together in the Guild and the Woman's Society that have brought me to this decision. I know that Doc hoped I'd go on working with him on "our research project"—as he called it—but I believe that teaching is where I belong. And I feel that my job is to teach in those parts of the world where there is a special need. I think this is what I've been searching for, only I just never realized it before.

ANN (*The two have stopped packing and look intently at one another across the "trunk."*): Doc and I quite agree, Martha. We've watched as you worked with the young people: how you have grown as you worked with them and with the women's groups, how your sense of mission has developed through teaching those migrants. Your dedication isn't just something you feel, it's become something you express. It's been your keen interest and enthusiasm that has convinced and inspired others.

MARTHA (*breaking in*): Oh, now, I'm not so special. It's just that I've finally found what I believe, and that belief leads me to do something active. There are lots of other folks here who are discovering this, too.

Do you remember, back when I was in college, the long session I had with you and Doc after the bombing of Hiroshima? I had plenty of questions even though I was only a student, or maybe because I was a student. Anyway, it was Doc who convinced me then that the atom could lead to revolutionary new ways of life, that it didn't have to be *only* destructive. I've found that many here who were working on the project had those same questions after they discovered what they had been working on.

ANN: That seems like such a long time ago, doesn't it? More than fifteen years. It's hard to imagine the changes that have taken place since then. There are still quite a lot of people here in Richland who came during those early days in the 1940's when this was hardly more than desert. Can you imagine what the original village of Hanford was like? Desert, four hundred people, and a tiny Methodist chapel. But the atom changed all that. And the Methodists were asked to sponsor this church as the first Protestant one in the community which the Atomic Energy Commission built. I know most of those who came here in those days weren't really aware of the tremendous implications of the project they were involved in. I'm sure many didn't realize that it would be used for death and destruction. Yes, it was quite a shock here, too. Perhaps it was this realization that set people to questioning what they really believed.

MARTHA: Yes, I think it encourages a growing understanding of the worth of life and of our Christian responsibility toward life. Perhaps working on this atomic project has sharpened people's awareness of the need for a real commitment. I do believe it has made them feel a greater need for a uniting spiritual force to counter the tremendous forces they work with. I suppose this may not be true in every community; and isn't it too bad that it sometimes takes the threat of destruction to bring people to their senses? It's been thrilling to be a part of this United Protestant effort . . . to see how people from so many different denominational backgrounds can find a unity in Christ and work together in harmony. As a good old solid Methodist I'm proud that our church has been so active in sponsoring this experiment in interdenominational cooperation and understanding.

ANN: Now that you've gotten a Wesleyan Service Guild going, I think we can begin to bring more women in our church into active participation in this big job we have; after all, it's going to take all of us working together to really make the church work. You know, one thing we women seem to enjoy is a problem or a project. We all need to be challenged to act as well as talk about our Christian experience.

MARTHA: Funny isn't it, how people react to a challenge? Remember two years ago when I was beating the bushes to find people to help us with that literacy class?

ANN: I had a letter from Nancy Conners just the other day, and she still recalls how you corralled her.

MARTHA: I remember I'd been pestering Jim for more names of more people I could contact, and he'd suggested the Conners; they hadn't been here very long. They weren't even members of the church although they had come with their daughter on several occasions. John Conners is a real farmer, isn't he? They've spent their life working on the land. He was with the water reclamation project up on the desert north of here before they retired. Strange that they're now out in Pakistan where I'm headed! I can see them now as they were when I burst in one afternoon just about two years ago. . . .

(Scene changes . . . Martha and Ann leave as John and

Nancy Conners enter. They can bring in a couple of lawn chairs to sit in. After they are seated, Martha re-enters.)

MARTHA: I'm Martha Wesley from Central Church. I met you the other evening at your daughter's. Jo Ann and I got to know each other in the Wesleyan Service Guild. I've come to you for help. Maybe you know that Central has taken the church down at the "Y," there where the highway divides, as a project. (*Martha sits down.*) Well, the people who live there have a real need for literacy classes, and I heard you've been a teacher, Mrs. Conners, and that you might be interested in helping. (*Martha is sitting on the edge of her chair; she finishes speaking breathlessly.*)

NANCY (*smiling at Martha*): Goodness, you sound as though there were a house on fire and you needed us to come help put it out!

MARTHA: It's not quite as urgent as a fire, but I must say those folks have a burning desire to learn. And I really do need help. You see, I'm no teacher; I just went down one time to see if there was anything I could do, and the next thing I knew I was sitting with a group of migrant laborers who were there; and because I knew a little Spanish, and they were Mexicans . . . well, there I was. (*She lifts her hands expressively.*) Many migrant workers stop off down there as they move from picking peas in Walla Walla to hops up by Prosser. Sometimes they're there for a few weeks, sometimes even for months. There are also quite a few Indian families who have moved off the reservation and now don't have much of any place to go. But they all, or almost all, are illiterate. Won't you come down and help us?

NANCY: Yes, I was a schoolteacher; but I don't know anything about teaching new literates. (*Turning toward her husband.*) Besides, John and I are thinking of going overseas. Washington State University has a technical team going to West Pakistan to help the government there with a water and power development project. We don't know just when we may be going, and so I hardly want to say I'll help if I don't know how long I can. Anyway, I'm already pretty busy with the University Women's Club. Perhaps you'd better find someone else.

MARTHA: Frankly, we'd be happy even if you came down once. But I don't want to urge you into doing something you wouldn't want. Maybe you'd just come and visit though. I think you'd be interested. Would you be able to come with me next week?

NANCY (*hesitantly*): Well . . . all right. It might be interesting. When do you go?

MARTHA: I'll pick you up a little after three on Tuesday. Now, will you excuse me? I've got about three more calls to make this evening. It's been nice having a chat with you. 'Bye, I'll see you on Tuesday. (*She finishes; waves as she leaves.*)

(*Nancy and John Conners sit looking at each other.*)

NANCY: Now, don't you look at me like that, John Conners! You know I've always been busy with the University Club or some civic group. And I'm just getting acquainted here. We wouldn't even have gone to church here if Jo Ann hadn't insisted. You know very well that we usually get fed up pretty quickly with most church groups where we've lived. They always seem so dead.

JOHN (*nodding his agreement*): I didn't say a thing. Maybe your conscience is bothering you. I must confess that usually you've been right. But this church seems different. In the first place it's a United Protestant Church—no hard-shelled denominationalists. Jo Ann said they'd been skeptical, too, at first. But now she says this is the first time they've been in a church where people from so many different backgrounds work together so harmoniously. Why don't you give this a try? You know you'd enjoy teaching, and you know you've got to be doing something or this "retirement living" will drive you nuts. (*He chuckles as Nancy bounds out of her chair.*)

NANCY (*finishing lamely and sitting down again*): Per-

TO DISCOVER

haps you're right . . . once in a while you are! I'll see. I did say that I'd go and visit. I must say it does get a bit lonesome, and I would sort of enjoy teaching. Maybe this would be fun. (*Both exit.*)

(*Lawn chairs, TV tables set up; John Conners stretched out in one as Martha and Nancy are talking as they enter.*)

MARTHA: You know, Nancy, you were hooked after that first visit to the literacy class. I'll admit it wasn't quite cricket, but I knew if I could get you to go, you'd help. Admit it, it does give you a grand feeling of being really useful, doesn't it? And I hear you really got the Woman's Society behind the project. We were lucky to have you to help us. And that training course you worked out was wonderful. Now we've got six teachers. It will take that many to replace you now that you and John are going to Pakistan. Why, you even managed to teach me to teach! (*Both laugh. They join John and sit down.*)

NANCY: I really can't thank you enough. If you hadn't kept after me like you did, I wouldn't have had such a wonderful experience this past year. In fact, it hardly seems like a whole year has gone by. You know, this is the first time in years that I've discovered that a church doesn't have to be full of stuffy people. Perhaps I was stuffy, too. But this year, after I got involved in the project and began to take part in the program of the Woman's Society, I think I've begun to find out what it means to try to act like a Christian. Imagine! At my age, and never found it out before.

MARTHA (*thoughtfully*): I know what you mean, Nancy. I've found something new and different here, too. Well, I know you won't lack for something to do when you get to Pakistan. Remember to keep us all posted. Let us know if there is anything we can do to help.

JOHN: How right you are. Nancy is always involved, but this is the first time in years that she's been, or I should say, we've been involved in a church. It's given us a new perspective. I must say, it's a challenge to see so many of you who are working daily to tap the energy of the atom finding such a meaningful experience in the church. There's no reason why others can't, too.

. . . .

Scene II

(*"Trunk" is removed; table in center with fruit bowl; either use wicker furniture or use chairs to simulate a couch; two or three chairs. Martha and Nancy enter, followed by John. He carries suitcases. Women have travel bags, etc.*)

MARTHA: Well, I do declare, Nancy and John. It was a surprise to see you two on the pier here in Karachi!

NANCY: Well, for goodness sakes, tell us how *you* happen to be here. I never dreamed when we left Richland that you'd be following us to Pakistan, least of all as a missionary! Well, I mean, I didn't imagine that a person with your training would be a missionary.

MARTHA (*laughing*): To tell the truth, I didn't either. It's quite a story. (*Sitting down.*) Oh, I say, this is like coming home. Sights, sounds, even smells are all so familiar. These cool concrete rooms, with their lazy ceiling fans. Even that bowl of fresh fruit seems like an old friend. Just like I remember things being when I spent those two years in north India on a Fulbright scholarship.

JOHN: That's right, I'd almost forgotten that you've been in these parts before.

NANCY (*going off stage, returns with tea tray, etc.*): We're about to move up country, so please excuse the mess in the house. Now, make yourself comfortable, and bring us up-to-date about yourself and everybody at home. (*She perches on a small reed stool, and John stretches out on the couch.*)

MARTHA: Where are you going? To Lahore?

JOHN: We're not exactly sure yet. But we just might be fairly near neighbors of yours.

TO DISCOVER

NANCY (*interrupting*): Come on. We can tell our news later. Martha, tell us how you happen to be here.

MARTHA: It began with those literacy classes. I got more involved after you left. (*Nancy pours tea, passes fruit, etc.*) One thing seemed to lead to another. Last summer I went to the Conference School of Missions . . . you know, the one sponsored by the Woman's Society. One of the studies was on migrants. Because of the literacy project I was particularly interested, so I took a week of my vacation in order to attend the whole conference. The other study was about Asia, and they emphasized the tremendous need for education of all sorts. It kept coming to mind all the rest of the summer, but every time I pushed it away. After all, I had a good job. The thought of going back overseas didn't impress me; my two years in India had been interesting, but I hadn't enjoyed the flies and dirt—and the disease! I saw too many Americans laid low because of some bug or other. Still, those summer classes got me to thinking.

NANCY (*questioningly*): What do you mean?

MARTHA: Well, I found myself wondering whether I should spend my time in a lab or with people. Not just that. I began to wonder if I couldn't be *more* useful as a teacher somewhere like India, or Pakistan, or Africa— somewhere where they needed teachers so badly.

JOHN: But, Martha, what you were doing was useful, too, wasn't it? Research you were doing will someday help many people.

MARTHA: Oh, you're right, John. But I began to feel that there might be a more direct way to share all those wonderful formulas and theories we spent days and months working out in the lab. There seemed to be a gap between what we were doing and what people needed. It wasn't just a matter of my job not accomplishing anything. You see, I discovered I liked to teach while helping in those literacy classes. And I began to feel that maybe I could make a better contribution by teaching than by working in a lab. I've enjoyed research . . . found it thrilling and challenging. But it suddenly didn't seem to satisfy me anymore. I felt that it wasn't enough just for me to be happy in my work. It seemed I ought to be making others happy, too. You know, Nancy, how it felt when we helped one of those folks in the literacy class learn to write his name? It wasn't even just a case of making them feel happier, but it was knowing that they were becoming better citizens, that they were coming closer to being the kind of "whole" person Rev. Jim was always saying we, as Christians, ought to be.

JOHN: You sound like we did thirty years ago. (*Nancy nods.*) A bit idealistic, perhaps, but we decided then that our contribution should be made in direct person-to-person contacts. For me, it meant working in the fields with farmers; for Nancy, it was teaching kids in school. Yes, we know something of what you mean. It's important to have people at the research and at the administrative side. And I'm coming to realize more and more how much they need to be dedicated Christians, too. But there's an awful lot of "grass roots" work to be done to help make this a better world.

NANCY: But Martha, this is a big gap in salary, isn't it? I'm sure what you got was a heap more than you'll get now as a missionary. Why didn't you come on a government contract or something that would offer a more comparable salary?

MARTHA: I decided that salary wasn't everything. It's not just the practical technology and American "know-how" which these people need, Nancy. To me, it became important to express and help people discover that God loves them. Just helping people isn't enough. I discovered that in those literacy classes . . . but even more while teaching that class of juniors in church school. For them, it's important that you *be* a Christian, not just talk about it! (*All exit.*)

.   .   .   .

TO DISCOVER

(*A year later, Martha, Nancy and a Pakistani woman enter. It is a village scene. They have just gotten out of a jeep [four chairs] and are gathering things to carry.*)

MARTHA: I don't see how you do it, Nancy. You bounce along in a jeep as if you'd done it all your life. I've been doing it once a week this entire year, coming out to the village for this literacy class, and I'm not used to it yet! And there you and John are. Living in a trailer house out in the desert, and at your age!

NANCY (*indignantly, but laughing*): What do you mean, "at my age"! Neither John nor I have reached seventy-five yet.

PREM: You two stop fussing. Come, we'll go first to the pastor's house. They will be expecting us. This is a big day, you know, for all the village. The twelve who will today receive certificates saying they can read and write will be the first adults in this village to do so.

NANCY (*gathering up a bundle*): Remember how suspicious they were the first time we came?

MARTHA (*reflectively*): Who would have thought that we would be teaching in literacy classes like this, Nancy? Remember, Prem, I told you how Nancy and I and others from our church at home used to go once a week, just like we three have been doing here, to teach farm laborers to read and write English. Interesting, isn't it? This literacy class sponsored by the West Pakistan Christian Council is so much like our literacy class for migrants at home.

PREM: These people are farmers, too. Only I think they are some different from those you told me about since these people do not move around so much like your "migrants," do you call them?

NANCY: Besides working together across denominational lines we cross national boundaries, too. Look, Prem, you're an Anglican . . . we call it Episcopalian at home . . . and we're Methodists, and Mr. Fraser is a Scotch Presbyterian. Bob Webber, who helped us prepare our literacy booklets, is a Southern Baptist from the United States, and Ann Roy, who also worked with us, is from the Congregational Church in England. Gracious, how international and ecumenical can you get!

(*They all laugh and move through a narrow walkway—place several chairs back-to-back to form walkway.*)

NANCY: Look up there on the rooftops! (*Points up.*) Women and children perched to get a better view. Those flat rooftops are perfect grandstand seats.

PREM: This is a big event. Look over there. (*Points to corner.*) All the village council are sitting, looking very dignified smoking their hookahs. (large pipes) Mr. Fraser said one of them had asked to learn to read and write. It would be wonderful if we can get the support of the leaders in the village.

MARTHA (*whispering to the other two*): Oh, those must be some of Farida's Muslim friends come to see her get her certificate. A whole group of women, looking like silent ghosts, sitting there all covered from head to foot in their white bourgahs. I'm so glad they are interested.

NANCY: Shhh! Prem, you'll have to interpret for me so I'll know what Pastor Massey says.

PREM: Yes. He is standing now. He says, "This is a big day for us. We welcome all our friends. Many people in far countries have been interested in helping our village. Some sent money. Some came themselves. Every week Miss Wesley and Mrs. Conners have come to help; they are from America. Every week Sister Prem has come. On the day when she does not work in the big hospital she comes here to help us. This is not their regular job. They come to do this because they believe that God loves us, and so we should love one another. To show this, they come to help us learn to read and write."

MARTHA: There's our class. Dada (Grandfather) and his son and his granddaughter, and Rhamat, our Muslim who never showed us her face until we'd been here a dozen times. And then it was only at her home where she invited us for tea. And the others, all women, either carrying a child on a hip or trailing several behind.

NANCY: Look at their faces! Why, they fairly glow. Like lanterns, they are. How wonderful to know we helped.

MARTHA (*quietly*): Yes, to see people's faces change because they now have had a new doorway opened to them. Surely this is helping God's kingdom. God means for each of us to be our best. And how can they be unless they learn? And how can they learn unless someone comes to teach them?

PREM: Remember those verses in Ephesians, Martha? "Spare no effort to make fast . . . the unity which the Spirit gives." Each of us has been given his gift . . . to equip God's people to work in his service. That's what we've been doing: using our gifts to equip others. You have showed me, too. If you, as foreigners, can give time to help, I can, too. It doesn't matter that we are from different countries . . . or even from different churches. The important thing is not what we've done, but that we did it in the love and in the name of Jesus Christ. We have all reached a bit closer to the unity we should have as Christians.

MARTHA: Nancy, we began "where the atom was split," and we were part of a church, united. At home we found a common challenge when we worked together as Christians. Because of our experiences there, we grew and so have been able to come halfway around the world to share with farm people in Pakistan what we first learned to share with migrants there: Christian love and concern as well as reading and writing. All together we are part of Christ's church. Why can't we always work together in this unity instead of letting our differences divide us? Men will still go on trying to channel the power of the atom. We must go on trying to be channels of the power of God's love to all men everywhere.

.   .   .   .

TO DISCOVER

PUT YOURSELF HERE (Have the group consider the following):
1. What do you know about Protestant cooperation in your community? Roman Catholic and Protestant, Jewish and Christian, other?
2. Do you think this plan of church unity would work in your community? Why? Why not?
3. Since you know from this section that Martha goes overseas as a missionary, consider why you think she went. Then go on and compare your reasons with hers.

RESOURCES

ORDER THE FOLLOWING FROM THE SERVICE CENTER
7820 READING ROAD, CINCINNATI, OHIO 45237

Methodist Church Related Vocations and Service Projects. A directory of opportunities for service offered by The Methodist Church. (EB) 15 cents each; 10 for $1.00; 100 for $9.00. (This pamphlet refers to vocations in the fields of music, world mission, ministry, business and editorial, education, mass communication, deaconess, short term projects, and hospitals and homes.)

Something to Share. Pamphlet on missionary and deaconess service prepared especially for young people interested in missionary service. For distribution in limited quantities. Free.

Men and Women Overseas. Outlines opportunities for service. 8 pages. Free.

Single Men and Women as US-2's and Overseas 3's. Information about special term mission service. 8 pages. Free.

Called to Mission. Leaflet for recruitment of missionaries. Free.

Peace Corps and Special Term Opportunities for Service. Mimeographed pamphlet explaining differences between Peace Corps and Special Term Opportunities for Service, and opportunities in both. Free.

Present. General interpretative pamphlet geared toward recruitment of college students. Free.

Free leaflets in the "**Methodist Work in New Nations**" series: **Pakistan.**

TO DISCOVER

The Attractive American. Points up the opportunity for families going abroad to make a Christian contribution toward international understanding. 35 cents.

Music from the New Nations. (Available from Service Center and Cokesbury.) A 12-inch 33⅓ rpm record of folk music, patriotic music, and Christian hymns demonstrating the cultural and spiritual vitality of new nations in Africa and Asia. Explanatory notes on jacket. (BOM) Sale only $5.00.

ORDER FROM
OFFICE OF PUBLICATION AND DISTRIBUTION
NATIONAL COUNCIL OF CHURCHES,
475 RIVERSIDE DRIVE, NEW YORK, N.Y. 10027

The National Council of Churches: What It Is; What It Does. 15 cents.

FOR SPECIFIC INFORMATION AND QUESTIONS, YOU MAY WRITE TO THE SOURCES LISTED BELOW:

for general information, literature, etc., write to Dr. John Johannaber, Office of Missionary Personnel, 475 Riverside Drive, Room 1373, New York, N.Y. 10027.

for high school students and pre-senior college students; information about vocational opportunities at home and abroad, how to prepare for a missionary vocation, and summer opportunities during college years, and any other information, write to Miss Joyce Gillilan, same address as above.

for Overseas-3 Program or for professionally qualified women, write to The Reverend Avery Manchester, same address as above.

for couples for career service, write to Dr. M. O. Williams, same address as above.

for U.S.-2's and deaconess candidates write to Miss Allene Ford, same address as above.

MISSIONARY ITINERATION:

for information about how to get a missionary to speak at your church, and for much other information related to his visit, see the excellent little pamphlet **Your Church and the Missionary Visitor.**

Order free from the Service Center (except for postage and handling in quantities: 20 copies, 25 cents; 50 copies, 45 cents; 100 copies, 65 cents.)

for a "Speakers List" of names and addresses of missionaries on furlough (or retired, or nationals on leave), write to your Conference Secretary of Missionary Education and Service. ("Speakers List" issued Jan., May, Sept.) List of Conference Secretaries can be found in the Directory of the Woman's Division; order from Service Center. 50 cents.

ABOUT THE AUTHOR: See "The World Our Parish"

to Create...

> a new climate
> of acceptance
> for all who stumble,
> but struggle for
> maturity

Journey to Acceptance

BEVERLY CHAIN

PURPOSES: To understand the nature of separation and acceptance in our lives.

To stimulate self-acceptance.

To stimulate acceptance of others.

PRE-PROGRAM PLANNING:

This is a difficult program. It will take time to prepare and time to rehearse. If you are not willing to spend time on it, you may choose to have the women read in advance some of the materials presented here, and at the meeting have only the exhibit, one of the filmstrips mentioned, discussion, and a brief time of worship. Do not attempt this program as it is written without rehearsal!

1—Decide which of the scenes you might want to dramatize and which will be read by hidden voices. Assign parts and rehearse. It might be a good idea, if your group is large, to have one group responsible for the exhibit and materials and another group responsible for the dramatizations under a second leader. Be sure the two groups have at least one rehearsal together.

2—Be sure that you will have a good record player, an extension cord, and the appropriate music ready for the meeting if you should wish to use the music as suggested at the beginning and middle of the program.

3—Be sure you have a filmstrip projector, a second extension cord, a spare bulb, a stand for the projector, and someone designated to operate it and to turn the lights on and off at the proper time if you use the filmstrip.

4—If you wish to use filmstrips, order from Cokesbury Film Depositories of your Regional Service Center (a) **Face to Face**—33⅓ rpm record with filmstrip. It portrays complexities of older youth-young adult life in urban culture. Color, sale, postage extra, $10.00. (b) **Members One of Another**—reading script. It presents subject of interpersonal relationships and what motives help us become real persons. Color, sale, postage extra, $5.50.

TO CREATE

5—If your group is quite large and/or ambitious, the entire program could be presented visually and on tape. A member of the group or a husband with a single lens reflex camera could take close-up pictures from magazines and from the exhibit that would be appropriate to illustrate the various scenes. *Use color film for slides.* Cost for 36 will be about $6.00 for film and developing. It will take about a week to get the slides back from the developer.
6—If one of the members of the group has a tape recorder, after some rehearsal the group could meet to record the dramatic scenes on tape. These can be used at the meeting instead of live voices. Whether you do it live or on tape, it is still a good way to rehearse.
7—For an interesting exhibit which might be used in conjunction with this program, see the resources at the end of the program.

You have been given a number of alternatives in preparing this program. The techniques and the order you choose will determine what the final program will be. The leader and the reader should be in front of the group throughout the presentation and might have speaker's stands with lights on each side of the room.

ACTION GROWING OUT OF THE PROGRAM:

1—Individual members in the group may decide to try to make friends by letting some person who has been alienated or ignored know that he is now accepted.
2—For insight, personal fellowship, and enjoyment, several members may decide to meet at intervals for play readings, discussions of modern literature, or films which portray the condition of modern man.

PROGRAM PRESENTATION:

Scene I

READER: There is a woman on the next street. She . . . well . . . her husband left her—if she ever had a husband. She screams all day at her dirty, crying child.
VOICE I: I don't know how she got into our neighborhood!
VOICE II: She didn't as far as I'm concerned.
VOICE III: If we all ignore her, maybe she will go away.
VOICE II: Fat chance! What would she go on?
VOICE III: The police could make her move. I mean, I'm sure she's . . . well, there must be a law.

TO CREATE

VOICE II: We don't have anything legal against her.
VOICE III: Well, what's a decent Christian woman to do?
READER: (Reads John 8:1-11).

Scene II

VOICE I: Lovely party, Janet. The way you've done over this room is just divine.
JANET: Thanks, Katie. That's a real compliment coming from you. Excuse me a moment, will you? I think there's an emergency in the kitchen.
VOICE I: Poor Janet. She tries so hard, but there's always something missing. This room—she spent so much money, but it just doesn't quite come off. A little gauche, don't you think? I mean, I'd never say anything to her—she's my best friend. But if I had her money, I'm sure I could do a little more with it.
VOICE II: I know what you mean. Poor Janet.
READER: "... there is something in the misfortune of our best friends which does not displease us. Who amongst us is dishonest enough to deny that this is true also of him? Are we not almost always ready to abuse everybody and everything, although often in a very refined way, for the pleasure of self-elevation, for an occasion for boasting, for a moment of lust? To know that we are ready is to know the meaning of the separation of life from life, and of 'sin abounding.'" (From *The Shaking of the Foundations* by Paul Tillich. Charles Scribner's Sons, New York, 1948. Page 157.)

Scene III

LEADER: Modern literature is full of the record of separation in our lives. In the following passage from Arthur Miller's *After the Fall,* a husband and wife, Quentin and Louise, give us some insight into the separation in their lives.
LOUISE: Everybody notices it, Quentin.
QUENTIN: What?

TO CREATE

LOUISE: The way you behave toward me. I don't exist. People are supposed to find out about each other. I am not all this uninteresting. Many people, men *and* women, think I *am* interesting.
QUENTIN: Well, I . . . (*He breaks off.*) I . . . don't know what you mean.
LOUISE: You have no conception of what a woman is.
QUENTIN: But I do pay attention . . . just last night I read you my whole brief.
LOUISE: Quentin, do you think reading a brief to a woman is talking to her?
QUENTIN: But that's what's on my mind.
LOUISE: But if that's all that's on your mind, what do you need a wife for?
QUENTIN: Now what kind of a question is that?
LOUISE: Quentin, that's the question!
QUENTIN (*afer a slight pause, with fear, astonishment*): What's the question?
LOUISE: What am I to you? Do you . . . do you ever *ask* me anything? Anything personal?
QUENTIN (*with rising alarm*): But Louise, what am I supposed to ask you? I *know* you!
LOUISE: No. (*She stands with dangerous dignity.*) You don't know me. (*Pause. She proceeds now with caution.*) I don't intend to be ashamed of myself any more. I used to think it was normal, or even that you don't see me because I'm not worth seeing. But I think now that you don't really see any woman. Except in some ways your mother. You do sense her feelings; you do know when she's unhappy or anxious, but not me. Or any other woman.

.   .   .   .

Quentin?
(*He is silent.*)
Silence is not going to solve it any more, Quentin. I can't live this way.
 (*After the Fall*, Arthur Miller. Copyright © 1964

TO CREATE

by Arthur Miller. Reprinted by permission of the Viking Press, Inc.)

LEADER: We see another kind of separation in Tad Mosel's play *All the Way Home,* based on James Agee's novel *A Death in the Family.*

MARY: Oh, Jay, sometimes I pray . . .

JAY: That's your privilege.

MARY: Now I can't say what I was going to say.

JAY: I'm listening.

MARY: But you're keeping your distance. As you always do when these things come up. There's a space of about a hundred miles between us.

JAY: And you've got that pursed-*up* look. That preachy pursed-up look.

(*There is an awkward silence. Neither one gives in. Finally she goes to him.*)

MARY: When the baby comes, it'll be time enough for him to hear about it, Jay. (*She puts her arms around his waist and leans against him. He does not respond.*)

JAY: Sure, Mary.

MARY: (*Stepping back, hurt, going to the kitchen.*) I thought we'd all have a glass of something cold before we start.

(*He bangs his pipe loudly into the ashtray while she gets the lemonade pitcher from the icebox. She stops in the middle of the kitchen and closes her eyes.*)

O Lord, in thy mercy, Who can do all things, close this gulf between us. Make us one in Thee as we are in earthly wedlock. For Jesus' sake. Amen.

(From *All the Way Home.* Copyright © 1961 by Tad Mosel. Reprinted here by permission of Ivan Obolensky, Inc.)

Instead of, or in addition to the above you may want to use frames 21-26 of the Methodist filmstrip, *Face to Face.*

READER: ". . . how strange we are to each other, how estranged life is from life. Each one of us draws back

TO CREATE

into himself. We cannot penetrate the hidden centre of another individual; nor can that individual pass beyond the shroud that covers our own being. Even the greatest love cannot break through the walls of the self."

(From *The Shaking of the Foundations* by Paul Tillich. Charles Scribner's Sons, New York, 1948.)

Scene IV

LEADER: We are separated from others because we are separated from ourselves.

VOICE I: I'm separated from myself. "I'm searching for a face . . . I do not mean the set of features on the surface of the head: the made-up mouth or the well-shaped brow, the ear-ringed ear . . . I don't mean the contour of the body but of being. The face of *me*: ears that hear . . . a mouth that can convey the inside out . . . and do it with integrity. Integrity? As what? I know I am, but what am I. Ah . . . that's the question!" (From *Face to Face*.)

VOICE II: I know what I am . . . I'm a housewife. I mean, that's what you say, isn't it? I'm a housewife, I'm mother to my children, and Mrs. Brown to the grocer, and Nancy to my friends, but do they know me? How can they? I hardly know myself. Where can I find myself? At the bottom of a pile of dishes or a stack of dirty laundry? In a woman's magazine? At the movies? In church? Where is the real me?

VOICE III (*with a suffering bewilderment*): Why am I afraid to dance, I who love music and rhythm and grace and song and laughter? Why am I afraid to live, I who love life and the beauty of flesh and the living colors of earth and sky and sea? Why am I afraid of love, I who love love? Why am I afraid, I who am not afraid? Why must I pretend to scorn in order to pity? Why must I hide myself in self-contempt in order to understand? Why must I be so ashamed of my strength, so proud of my weakness? Why must I live in a cage like a criminal, defying and hating, I who love peace and friendship? Why was I born without a skin, O God, that I must wear armor in order to touch or to be touched? Or rather, Old Graybeard, why the devil was I ever born at all?

(Copyright 1926 and renewed 1954 by Carlotta Monterey O'Neill. Reprinted from *Nine Plays By Eugene O'Neill* by permission.)

LEADER: We are separated from ourselves because we are separated from God. In current society we find it embarrassing even to speak of God except in profanity or in debate. In *Wild Strawberries,* the Swedish film maker, Ingmar Bergman, sums up the modern position:

ANDERS: "Oh, when such beauty shows itself in each facet of creation, then how beautiful must be the eternal source of this emanation!"

SARA: Anders will become a minister and Viktor a doctor.

VIKTOR: We swore that we wouldn't discuss God or science on the entire trip. I consider Anders' lyrical outburst as a breach of our agreement.

SARA: Oh, it was beautiful!

VIKTOR: Besides, I can't understand how a modern man can become a minister. Anders isn't a complete idiot.

ANDERS: Let me tell you, your rationalism is incomprehensible nonsense. And you aren't an idiot either.

VIKTOR: In my opinion the modern . . .

ANDERS: In my opinion . . .

VIKTOR: In my opinion a modern man looks his insignificance straight in the eye and believes in himself and his biological death. Everything else is nonsense.

ANDERS: And in my opinion modern man exists only in your imagination. Because man looks at his death with horror and can't bear his own insignificance.

VIKTOR: All right, religion for the people. Opium for the aching limb. If that's what you want.

SARA: Aren't they fantastically sweet? I always agree with the one who's spoken last. Isn't this all extremely interesting?

TO CREATE

VIKTOR (*angry*): When you were a child you believed in Santa Claus. Now you believe in God.
ANDERS: And you have always suffered from an astonishing lack of imagination.

(*Four Screenplays of Ingmar Bergman,* Essandess Paperback, Simon and Schuster, Inc., 1965, pages 202, 203. Used by permission of Janus Films Inc., Cambridge, Mass.)

LEADER: We have forgotten God and substituted other gods: money, success, joy, youth. That is the reason for our separation; and if God should choose suddenly to speak to us, the conversation might very well sound like this one from Paddy Chayefsky's *Gideon*.

THE ANGEL: Gideon, do you not know me? It is hardly four generations since Moses. Do not the young men know my name any more? I am your Lord Yahweh, the Kinsman of Jacob, who was the father of all the houses in Israel.

GIDEON: I have heard the old men talk of My Lord Yahweh.

THE ANGEL: Well, I am he.

GIDEON: I shall not say you are not.

THE ANGEL: I tell you I, even I, am he!

GIDEON: Pray, sir, do not shout.

THE ANGEL: What a stiff-necked fellow you are!

GIDEON (*thoroughly distressed*): What would you have me say? I am a poor farmer, beating out wheat in his wine press. Suddenly, a black-bearded stranger appears at my elbow and shouts at me: "I am your God." Well, I find this all an unusual business. I do not hold everyday traffic with gods. I said: "Very well." What else should I have said? And you have abused me roundly and hold me back from my pressing work.

THE ANGEL: I did not mean to discomfort you.

GIDEON: And now that I am put to it, I will tell you plainly . . . I do not believe in gods. I am not all as witless as my fellows sometimes think me. I have thought

TO CREATE

about these matters lately, and I do not believe in gods. You say that you are the god, Yahweh. The fact is, sir, in these parts, you are but a minor divinity. When I was a boy, you were more highly thought of, I think. But we Abiezrites are poor men, hill farmers. Our soil is hard, and we must pray for fertility, so we adopted a goddess with breasts and a womb, Ishtar—a sportive lady, I must say; her festivals are lively times. A farmer, you see, needs a romping God. And Yahweh, as I recall, was grim. Oh, sir, we have had all manner of gods here—the Bull-El, Yam, Mot, pin-breasted Ashtartes, Anu, Anath, the Mother Goddess of the wonderful womb, and now we have added the rain Ba-al of Beth-shean! And to all these gods I gave my full and primitive awe. I truly, truly served them. For I am a child in many ways and truly thought the wind did love me, and that the thunder was angry at something I did, and that I sliced our poor Lord Ba-al in half as I sickled my wheat, for such is the story, you know, that Ba-al dies each year at the harvest. How I wailed as I reaped! I truly, truly thought the air was cluttered with fierce powers. But lately I have come to wondering.

. . . .

LEADER: Gideon moves quickly from wondering to knowing that he cannot accept God.
THE ANGEL: Are you suggesting some sort of divorce between your God and you?
GIDEON: We make an ill-matched pair, my Lord. You surely see we never meet but tempers rise between us. It is too much for me, this loving God. I cannot manage it. I am a plain man and subject to imperfect feelings. I shall betray you many times, and you shall rise in wrath against me and shall punish me with mighty penalties, and I cannot continue in this way, my Lord. Oh, let me say it plainly. I do not love you, Lord, and it is unreasonable to persist with each other when there is no love.
THE ANGEL (*startled*): You do not love me?

GIDEON: I tried to love you, but it is too much for me. You are too vast a concept for me. To love you, God, one must be a god himself. . . . Let me go, God.

THE ANGEL: Let you go—whatever does that mean? Gideon, there is no divorce from God. I am truth and exist. You cannot deny that I am. I stand palpably here before you, as real as rock, a very actual thing with whom you have commerced face-to-face.

GIDEON: Aye, my Lord. I see you and hear you. So I beg of you, my Lord—Go from my sight. Make not your presence known to me again that I might say: "God is a dream, a name, a thought, but not a real thing."

THE ANGEL: But I am a real thing.

GIDEON: I would pretend that you were not. (THE ANGEL *is a little startled at this.*)

THE ANGEL: Let me review this. You would pretend God is not, although you know that he is, so that you might be a significant creature which you know you are not. Oh! This is beyond even God's understanding!

. . . .

You want the universe to please your eye, Gideon, and not mine. You would be God yourself. Hear me well, O Hebrew. I am a jealous God and brook no other gods, not even you. Why have I come here at all but to put an end to false idols? You have done well in pulling down the effigies of Ba-al, but do not think to set yourself up on their empty altars. Do not make a cult of man, not even in fancy.

. . . .

GIDEON: O God! I cannot believe in you! If you love me, let me believe at least in mine own self! If you love me, God!

(© 1961, 1962 by Carnegie Productions, Inc. Reprinted with deletions from *Gideon* by Paddy Chayefsky, by permission of Random House, Inc.)

TO CREATE

READER: ... we as men know that we are separated. We not only suffer with all other creatures because of the self-destructive consequences of our separation, but also know *why* we suffer. We know that we are estranged from something to which we really belong, and with which we *should* be united. We know that the fate of separation is not merely a natural event like a flash of sudden lightning, but that it is an experience in which we actively participate, in which our whole personality is involved ...
LEADER: Now let us look down into ourselves to discover there the struggle between separation and reunion, between sin and grace in our relation to others, in our relation to ourselves and in our relation to the Ground and aim of our being. (*The Shaking of the Foundations*, Tillich.)

Music: You may wish to use a classical record such as César Franck's *Symphony in D Minor*. Play it a full five or ten minutes. Give the women time to look into themselves.

Discussion: At the close of the period of meditation, the leader may suggest that the group divide into smaller groups of about five persons to discuss the exhibit, if it is used, and aspects of separation and acceptance in their own lives.
LEADER: (*When the group has come together again.*)
God calls us to acceptance.
We are accepted.
The moment we recognize our need acceptance is there.
We cannot transform our lives, but we can allow them to
    be transformed.
Consider Saul.
READER: Acts 9:1-22.

LEADER: We cannot transform our lives, unless we allow them to be transformed by that stroke of grace. It happens; or it does not happen. And certainly it does *not* happen if we try to force it upon ourselves, just as it shall not happen so long as we think, in our self-complacency, that we have no need of it.

(*The Shaking of the Foundations*, Tillich).

Scene V

VOICE I: Grace . . . Acceptance? What can it mean? I accept people . . . I accept people every day . . . I have to. There's no other way to live. Whom do I accept? Well . . . the people I work with . . . and my neighbors and my family. You mean I should accept someone else. Someone less than I?

VOICE II: Yes, of course, I can be charitable to the unemployed, the divorcée, the person in analysis, the alcoholic —maybe even a prostitute if I knew one.

You didn't mean charity? Acceptance is different? Yes . . . Well . . What? A woman with a prison record? A Negro as an equal? Someone I find stupid? A person who never seems to wash? Isn't that taking acceptance a bit too far?

VOICE III: Accept someone more than I am? The woman with the mink? The one who beats me at bridge every time? The woman with that beautiful house in the country and another at the lake? All those people who seem to be healthier and happier and more talented? Why do they need my acceptance?

VOICE IV: Accept life? But of course I do! My mother-in-law? My aged aunt? But they're so difficult! Other people's children? The war in Vietnam? Kindness? Beauty? That's a strange mixture!

Oh! You mean that I should see life whole. Accept the good and bad together. I shall have to think about that a bit.

VOICE I: There's more to this acceptance than I thought . . . so much to accept. God, myself, life, others. So difficult to find the meaning.

(Your group may elect to use the filmstrip, *Members*

TO CREATE

One of Another, which explores several aspects of acceptance; or read excerpts from it. See script which accompanies filmstrip, frames 4-47).

VOICE II: A face behind the mask. But who could love me if they saw me as I really am . . .? How could I love myself . . .? The darkness there . . . the boiling up of hate and envy . . . the animal appetites . . . the fears . . . who would admit to the fear of inadequacy . . . the terror of rejection . . . the horror of death . . . No one could love me as I really am!

VOICE III: Ah—but what are you really—all of it . . . the rest behind the mask? . . . so much more you are ashamed to show. That terrible need to find meaning in what I do . . . That driving hunger to be of authentic use . . . Yes, and even that capacity to sacrifice . . . and suffer . . .

VOICE II: And that wild ache to find someone wiser, stronger, superior to our human need. These things in you . . . in you, too? Of course in me, in you, in all of us . . . We're human beings and this is what it is to be in human flesh . . . But it is something more as well. For God so loved us, He Himself invaded human flesh . . . He became what we are that we might become what He is.

VOICE III: If we expose ourselves to Him, give up ourselves to Him, the masks must fall away . . . For he will grow us as He means for us to grow—toward Sonship. In Him, our real selves wait for us!

(*Face to Face,* frames 82-90).

READER: Grace strikes us when we are in great pain and restlessness. It strikes us when we walk through the dark valley of a meaningless and empty life. It strikes us when we feel that our separation is deeper than usual, because we have violated another life, a life which we loved, or from which we were estranged. It strikes us when our disgust for our own being, our indifference, our weakness, our hostility and our lack of direction and composure have become intolerable to us. It strikes us when, year after year, the longed for perfection of life does not appear, when the old compulsions reign within us as they have for decades, when despair destroys all joy and courage. Sometimes at that moment a wave of light breaks into our darkness, and it is as though a voice were saying: "You are accepted. *You are accepted,* accepted by that which is greater than you, and the name of which you do not know."

(*The Shaking of the Foundations,* Tillich. Pages 161-162.)

VOICE I: I accept the fact that I am accepted. I may not be better than before, I may not believe more than before, but now reconciliation bridges the gulf of estrangement. I am accepted and nothing is demanded of this experience but my acceptance.

VOICE II: I accept the power to perceive myself in relation to others. I accept the grace of being able to look frankly in another's eyes and to understand his words and what lies behind his words even when they are harsh and angry. I accept the reunion of life with life.

VOICE III: I accept the power to say "yes" to myself, to experience peace instead of hate or self-contempt.

VOICE I: I accept the fact that I am accepted.

Prayer: The prayer should grow out of the individual life of the group and their reaction to the program. Do not write in advance a prayer to be read. Someone should be asked in advance to be prepared to lead the group in prayer. Such a prayer would contain praise and thanks to God, petitions for those persons from whom we have alienated ourselves, forgiveness for wrongs we have done, and thanks for God's acceptance in spite of our unworthiness. One of the assignments for the discussion period might be to work out elements of this common prayer.

Hymn: The closing hymn should be one of joy. Have the group sing together a hymn which they know well and can sing with ease. Some possibilities might be

TO CREATE

"O For a Thousand Tongues to Sing," "Praise to the Lord, the Almighty, the King of Creation," or "Now Thank We All Our God." (*The Methodist Hymnal*)

. . . .

Exhibit: Have a program committee meeting to prepare the exhibit. Even with a number of women to work on it, this will take three or four hours. A stack of *Life* and *Look* magazines, scissors, rubber cement, the poster boards and lettering tools are essential. The lettering should be done on separate paper or cardboard, then pasted to the poster board so that one error does not ruin the total poster. Purchase twenty large sheets of heavy poster board (eight black and twelve white). These should be about two feet by three feet in size. You should have about sixteen panels in your exhibit (eight on separation and eight on acceptance.) Themes of the various panels could be: acceptance of self and its opposite, acceptance of someone more than yourself, someone rejected by society, life in its daily trying aspects, a world in revolt, God. (See below for a list of suggested titles and photographs). The pictures on the panels should tell the story. The words used should be very few and to the point. Work out a good way to display the exhibit. You may want to use clothespins and pin the panels to two strips of wire, one on either side of the room, or on one side and across the front of the room. The panels could serve as the backdrop for your stage later in the program.

SUGGESTED POSTER TITLES
FOR "ACCEPTANCE"

1. Who needs acceptance? (photo—delinquent)
2. Surely not me? (photo—well-dressed, poised woman)
3. When the going's tough . . . (photo—woman discouraged)

4. Where do you look for acceptance? (photos—movies, liquor, church, pills, coffee with neighbor)

5. And what do you give?

6. Love to her, maybe? (photo, Negro mother and child)

7. Or her? (photo, disagreeable woman.) What about the man who . . . (photo, disagreeable man)

8. Have you accepted yourself? (photo, woman looking in mirror)

9. Well, then there's GOD. . . .

SUGGESTED POSTER TITLES FOR "SEPARATION"

1. Separated? Not me! (photo, woman surrounded by children and adults)

2. Of course I can't stand that woman! (photo, woman; second photo, woman)

3. My husband doesn't know the real me. (photo, husband and wife)

4. What I'm like inside. (photo, woman looking at viewer)

5. I don't understand myself. (photo, woman working)

6. God? It's a little embarrassing to talk about God. (photo, group in front of church)

7. I guess it's the world we live in. (war photo)

8. Separation? Could be.

Plan questions which will help the members get the most out of the exhibit. Have them jot down the answers as they view the exhibit at the start of the meeting so that they will be ready to discuss them at the appropriate time. Some possible questions might be: What elements of acceptance and separation are revealed in this exhibit? What elements are missing? Which panel was most meaningful to you? Why? Be sure that a member of the program committee is in each discussion group to aid as leader or stimulator.

TO CREATE

ACCESSORIES

Order the following from the Wright Studio, 5624 Brookville Road, Indianapolis, Indiana 46219 (N.B. On orders less than $4.00, please add 25 cents for handling).

Christian Witness Puzzlemat. Gaily colored rebus placemat suggests need of Christians to bear witness to their faith and to reach out to others. 20 for 75 cents.

World Neighbor Dolls. Cardboard cutouts of people from around the world, each one in his own native costume and in color. Set of 12 dolls, $1.50.

ABOUT THE AUTHOR

For the past seven years, Miss Beverly Chain has been employed by RAVEMCCO, the Radio and Visual Education Mass Communications Committee of the Division of Foreign Missions of the National Council of Churches, as Director of Communication Services.

Previous to beginning work for RAVEMCCO, Miss Chain was Director of Promotion for the Evangelical Audio-Visual Center (CAVE) in Campinas, Brazil. She was appointed to this work as a special-term missionary of The Methodist Church.

Miss Chain is author of the book, *Days of Decision*, a collection of short stories about South America, published by Friendship Press. She has also written a number of filmstrip scripts including the "Christian Friends in Other Lands" series produced by Family Films. Many feature articles have appeared under her by-line in Christian magazines over the past six years. She has written programs for women and youth of The Methodist Church, the Reformed Church of America, and the Lutheran Church.

Miss Chain has a degree in journalism from Ohio University at Athens, Ohio, and a master of arts degree in communications from New York University. She is a member of the Religious Public Relations Council, and of Theta Sigma Phi, national fraternity for women in journalism. She is also an alumna of Kappa Phi, Methodist women's sorority, and was active in Wesley Foundation during her college years.

For All Who Stumble
(Operation Headstart)

SHARON FLYNN

PURPOSES: To give a personal reflection of one Operation Headstart teacher who taught preschool-age children in a poverty stricken area.

To stimulate local societies and guilds in accepting the challenge of sponsoring similar education programs in the local church.

PRE-PROGRAM PLANNING:

(1) The main portion of this program is a conversation between three young women. A narrator and two women will be needed. The worship can be led by one worship leader.

(2) Statistics and evaluations of Operation Headstart are available from the Office of Economic Opportunity, Washington, D. C. Books, magazines and newspaper articles will highlight Operation Headstart from time to time.

(3) You might want to compile a bibliography including the items mentioned in the supplementary materials and other more recent magazine and newspaper articles.

This could be available to the members of your society or guild prior to the meeting. If your church has a library, ask that such reading materials be made available.

(4) If there has been an Operation Headstart program in or near your community, you might consider securing one of the teachers from it to participate in this program, perhaps answering questions which arise should you have a discussion period following the program.

(5) If a decision is made to establish an Operation Headstart program and there are no local headquarters, write to the Office of Economic Opportunity, Washington, D. C., for application forms.

TO CREATE

ACTION GROWING OUT OF THE PROGRAM:

Investigate what can be done in your community to stimulate more effective participation, not only in Project Headstart and other government-sponsored antipoverty programs, but also in endeavors to solve other social problems.

PROGRAM PRESENTATION:

The earth is the Lord's and the fullness thereof, the world and those who live therein; . . . Know that the Lord is God! It is He that made us, and we are His; we are His people, and the sheep of His pasture. Enter His gates with thanksgiving, and His courts with praise! Give thanks to Him, bless His name! For the Lord is good; His steadfast love endures forever, and His faithfulness to all generations. (Psalms 24:1, 100:3-5, from the Revised Standard Version of the Bible. Copyrighted 1946 and 1952.)

HYMN: "Where Cross the Crowded Ways of Life." No. 465, *The Methodist Hymnal.*

PRAYER: (in unison): Lord, be with those who have little. Be with those of full lives. And be with those who are empty. For we are all thy children. And we need thy help to love one another.

NARRATOR: Operation Headstart is an aid to education made possible by the Economic Opportunity Act of 1964. Is is specifically designed to provide a "headstart" in the learning experiences for socially and economically deprived children before they enter public school. Today we will share in the experiences of two teachers who took part in Operation Headstart. They represent the large corps of volunteer workers, both paid and unpaid, who are working to see that all children in the United States have an equal opportunity to be exposed to those early childhood experiences which will help them in their social and personal development.

TO CREATE

(Marcy, Sarah, and Amy walk casually and quietly onto the stage. Marcy is carrying a tray with a coffeepot and three cups full of coffee. During the program they drink coffee from time to time. They walk over to three chairs which are grouped around a coffee table and then seat themselves, Marcy first setting the tray down on the coffee table. While they are walking over, the Narrator says:)

NARRATOR: Let's visit Marcy, Sarah and Amy, friends for many years. They are meeting for the first time in three months. Marcy and Sarah have been teaching in a summer Headstart program in a large near-by city.

AMY: How nice it is to have you two back again. I'm so anxious to hear about your adventures with the new government poverty program—what was it called? Operation Headstart? *(Marcy nods her head.)* I can't imagine what one could do in a program like that, or why it's necessary. My Jimmy went to kindergarten last year, and he got along fine. He didn't need any preschool program to help him get through.

MARCY: Of course he didn't, Amy. But you're not poor.

AMY: But we aren't rich either. We have a struggle to make ends meet, just like everybody else.

SARAH: Oh, Amy, I used to feel that way, too, until I visited some of the homes of my pupils in Headstart. In one home there were two beds for seven people: four of the children slept on one bare mattress—they had no sheets or blankets. The younger children spent the day naked from the waist down—they had no diapers.

MARCY: Yes, and in one home that I visited, there was no heating system of any kind. When I asked them what they did for heat in the winter, they said they turned on the jets of the gas stove. Imagine trying to keep warm in a room heated only by a few jets of gas from a stove.

AMY: Oh, I had no idea it was so bad! But those things can't be corrected in school; how does Operation Headstart help these children if it can't change the surround-

TO CREATE

ings they live in? It seems to me that all the children in my son's kindergarten were about the same. Some were noisier than others, and some were bigger, or smaller, or better dressed, but basically they all knew the same things.

SARAH: Yes, most children in most kindergartens do know basically the same things. They know the names of the things around them; they know colors, sizes, shapes; they all have a fairly large basic vocabulary; many of them can count a little, and some even know a few letters. But these are not the children of real poverty. I wish I could show you what some of their lives are like. Marcy, how do you explain it to someone who's never seen a really deprived family?

MARCY: Well, try to imagine a child who rarely says anything, not because he's dumb, and not because he's shy, but because no one ever talks to him at home so he's never learned any words. Oh, he may know a few words, like "Shut up"; but in his home people don't converse with one another, so he doesn't know what it is to talk with somebody.

SARAH: And I know one little boy who was being given an intelligence test and who failed many of the parts because he'd never been taught the names of colors, or the names of the things around him. Another child, when asked what color bananas were, answered, "Brown," because he had never seen a fresh yellow or green banana. And he couldn't hand the train to the examiner, which is another part of the test, because he didn't know what a train was.

AMY: Oh, how sad! I just hadn't realized what it was like. Don't these children have parents who love them? What is it that our children have that these children don't have?

MARCY: Basically, our children get more care, more attention, and more experiences. These children are so deprived that they may never have had anyone read them a story. Probably there are no magazines or newspapers

TO CREATE

in their homes; certainly there are few if any books. Perhaps the father, unable to support his growing family, has left home in utter discouragement, leaving a mother who must work constantly to provide the little her family has. She may love her children, but she hasn't the time or the energy, or the knowledge to teach them things, to take them on little trips around the city, to point out interesting things to them. Frequently the younger children are left in the care of an older child, who may not be much older than they are, and for whom child care is just too much.

AMY: But what did you do? Why did you have to work with them, anyway? Don't you do enough teaching in the winter? I know you teach kindergarten, Sarah, but weren't you nervous about dealing with such different children as these?

MARCY: Yes, but all the teachers and assistant teachers had been given a week's orientation, and, of course, I had aides and volunteers from the community helping me; but even so, I was a little anxious before I started; I really didn't know what to expect, and so I planned everything down to the last pot of paint. You should have seen me: room prepared, supplies ready, activities planned; I was nervous as a kitten and expecting everything and nothing. But I did feel that, whatever it was, something significant was going to happen. And at 8:00 in the morning I opened the doors and smiled.

AMY: What happened then?

MARCY: Well, a little dynamo named Lillie bounded into the room. She took one look around her and dived in, talking a mile a minute. In the next fifteen minutes she dressed and undressed the doll baby, set the table with vigor if not with neatness, and "painted" something on the easel that would have gladdened the heart of one of those modern abstract expressionist painters.

AMY: My goodness, that's not what I expected you to say. I thought all those poor children would be shy and fearful,

TO CREATE

and you'd have an awful time getting anything out of them.

SARAH: I know that all the children weren't like Marcy's Lillie. There were many others who almost crept into the room, their eyes roaming everywhere but on the teacher. These were the ones I was prepared for, too. I knew just what to do: I told each one what my name was, and then I asked what his name was. When he told me, I shook hands with him.

AMY: You shook hands with him? Isn't that awfully formal and adult for a child?

SARAH: I had to reach the shy children, and I hoped that by shaking hands—that is, by touching the child—I could make a beginning step toward establishing a relationship with him. These children are all too often completely neglected—no one even bothers to hug them or pick them up. When I shook hands, the child felt that I cared enough about him to touch him, and it was the first step in our reaching out toward each other. But it also gave me a chance to lead him to one of the activity areas of the room. Watching each child play was my first clue toward understanding that child.

AMY: Well, I've heard about play therapy, although I don't quite know what it is, but I don't see how you could learn much by watching a child play. All children play the same way: paint with the paints, play house with the dishes, build with the blocks.

SARAH: That's what I thought, too. But one of my first "lessons," so to speak, was Revell. He came into the room, picked up a truck, went to the sewing corner and got a basket of beads and some scissors, managed to put a box of blocks under one arm, and then went over to the toy cash register and sat down.

AMY: He sounds like a little troublemaker. You should have told him that the blocks stay in the block area, the beads in the game area, and so forth. He just must have wanted all those things for himself.

TO CREATE

SARAH: Well, something cautioned me to wait a few minutes before I tried to insist that he abide by the rules and leave each toy in its proper area. As I watched him, I suddenly realized that he had made up his own game, one that he could not play at home because there was nothing in his home for him to play with: he was playing store with the toys, and thoroughly enjoying something he must have longed to do in real life. But, of course, not all the children played in as meaningful a way as Revell.

AMY: Do you think any of this playing did any good? I realize that most of these children don't have toys in their own homes, but how can playing with toys help them?

SARAH: Well, for example, I think that the artistic forms of expression were important in the growth of the children. Let me tell you about Pamela. She was a silent child and played rather aimlessly. She had such trouble expressing what she felt inside. One morning Pamela picked up a brush, dipped it in the paint, and began painting a picture at the easel. I was overjoyed and asked her to tell me about the picture. She said that it was a picture of her family, and she named the members as Mother, Ronald, Rodney, Keith and Sharon. Significantly, she had left out Father. Pamela continued to paint this picture for several days. Then one day, as she painted, she began making heavy strokes through the picture. In a minute she was spattering paint on the floor and the wall in a real fit of temper. I approached her calmly and said that she was spattering paint and should not do that. As soon as I walked away, she picked up the brush and continued as before. When I asked what was bothering her, the reply was more spattered paint. Suddenly I realized that this was the release of an emotion she had repressed for a long time. She didn't consider her father worthy to be a member of the family. At the same time she did not like this picture of her family without him. When she finished blotting out the painting, I asked her to help me clean up, and she was quite agreeable. The

TO CREATE

rest of the morning she was happy, and she even skipped home. Pamela had learned something. She had dealt with life as she saw it in a symbolic way; now she could develop the ability to deal with it in a realistic way.

MARCY: And let me tell you what happened with three of my children. They actually learned, from their play, some of the meaningful rules of life: in this case, how to work together, and what to do when something goes wrong. There were two sisters, Eva and Verita, and their cousin Margaret. They spent almost their entire first week at the sink. They washed and rinsed the dishes, table, and doll babies a hundred times. They spilled water and soapsuds all over the floor. I thought it was necessary, though, to allow this play because these little girls had not previously had the opportunity to express themselves in this way. As they talked among themselves, I got the picture of their family life. Their father was a rigid disciplinarian, and the children had no voice in anything. Of course there was no play sink, and they were not allowed near the real sink. They couldn't even play together freely because an older sister had charge of them and was the boss in all play situations. I gradually encouraged these three to reduce the number playing in the sink at one time, to take turns with the soapsuds, and to mop up spilled water. Rules began to serve as an aid, rather than a hindrance. The children learned that when they imposed some rules upon themselves, their playing was easier and more enjoyable, and they could accomplish more. Their aimless play gradually grew into a dramatic re-enactment of family scenes. One day while playing house Verita, the youngest, was setting the table while her sister and cousin were preparing the food. As Margaret carried water from the sink to the table and tried to pour it into the cups, she spilled it all over, and the table became sopping wet. Verita loudly exclaimed, "You're making a mess, and now we can't eat. You don't eat water in a saucer, and besides, the water is on the floor." And just a week before, spilled water had meant nothing to them. Eva then said, "We better clean it up." And to my delight, Margaret, who had spilled the water, was helped by her sister and her cousin to mop up. Besides learning responsibility, they had learned how to play together and how to work together.

AMY: You know, I've been thinking about those children you mentioned before who talked in monosyllables, and who had such small vocabularies and such an inability to talk with people because no one talked to them at home. Did you have any specific ideas for working with them?

SARAH: Oh, yes, there were many, many things we did with language. Of course, I talked with them about what they were doing, or what they were building or making. Many times after we had talked about a specific object or event, the children would dictate a story to me. The printed story was hung on a bulletin board at their eye-level to serve as a reminder of the experience. Language development also depended on experiences outside the classroom. I think the best example was the word "construction." Most of the children in the Headstart program had walked past construction sites many times, but, generally speaking, no one had ever explained the process of construction or the names of the building materials. I decided to visit a nearby construction site with them. Before mentioning the trip, I began to use the word "construction" with the children in the block area and at the game tables. I pointed out pictures of construction in books. On the day of the trip we talked about construction before we left. At the site I pointed out mortar, wheelbarrow, cement truck and pulleys. Then we watched how the bricks were placed together at the top part of the building. When we returned to the classroom, we formed a discussion circle; and I asked the children what they had seen. Ernest responded with, "We went to see the school being built up." When I asked him what word he could use, someone else in the group piped up with "construction." Patty told the group about the string and ball she had seen lifting the bricks. This was her way of describing a pulley. After the discussion I printed their story about the trip. Whenever possible, I reread the story with the children.

SARAH: We took trips, too, to the butcher's, to a bakery, to public schools, to an art show, to the beach. But I think our best trip was the excursion to Staten Island on the ferry.

AMY: What made it your best trip?

SARAH: Well, before the trip, I read a story to the children about a lighthouse on the river. We talked about rivers, ferryboats, birds at sea, and so forth. On the ferry there were no happier children than Gregory announcing, "I see a buoy," Denise explaining, "That's a sea gull," and the cluster on deck proclaiming, "There's the lighthouse." The exposure to this world beyond their block had made geography personal. They saw the larger world and realized that buses, subways, and ferryboats were a means of taking them to other parts of this world; and they were really excited about this world.

MARCY: I think another one of the major activities was the medical program. The trips to the dentist and frequent visits from the doctor demonstrated to the parents that other persons cared about and served their children. It was a little more difficult to convince the children that the dentist and doctor meant help and not harm. It took a long time to quell Maria's fear of the needle. Maria was such a lively, curious child that I was surprised when she cried at the dental clinic. We didn't force her to have an examination. The second trip was less difficult for her, but she still resisted the examination; and I was determined to let her go at her own rate. By the third visit, she had worked up enough courage to inform me that she wasn't afraid any more. My praise of the decision, coaching from her classmates, and a smiling dentist managed to get her through her first examination. She proudly announced that it didn't hurt, and that she was coming back again.

AMY: I can see the terrific strides these children made. They must have a lot of potential growth which can be tapped through Operation Headstart.

MARCY: Yes, they have. I would say there are three main things this program does: it gives individual attention to each child, sometimes the first such attention he's ever had; it gives the child opportunities for free and creative growth in understanding himself; and it provides invaluable experience both inside and outside the classroom in language development. When these children came into the program, they needed a lot of help; now they're started on the way toward standing on their own.

SARAH: Yes, these children have tremendous resources of their own, but these resources have been repressed or halted because of their home backgrounds and because of the public school's neglect of preschool education.

AMY: This sounds like something our Woman's Society or Guild could do. Is there any way such a group could help?

SARAH: I wonder why I didn't think of that. It's a fine idea. Churches all over the country are being used as centers for Operation Headstart programs. And housewives are needed to work in the centers as aides and volunteers, for many kinds of women other than certified teachers are needed to serve. Do you think maybe we could do some investigating about what is needed in our local situation? (*The three women nod agreement and get up, going out together while still talking about what they can do in Operation Headstart.*) As they leave the stage, the Narrator says: Who are the deprived people in our community? And are there different kinds of deprivation? What can we do to help our community today before it grows any later?

PRAYER (in unison): O God, we cannot come before Thy face in this day with paltry little prayers. We ask only the grace to give all that we are and have, that Thy will may be done on earth. Forgive us the triviality and pettiness of our efforts for good before the magnitude of evil. Bind us inextricably with all Thy children. Lift our hearts, clarify our vision and strengthen our hands to do Thy work that we may be worthy to be called Thy children. Amen.

HYMN: "Once to Every Man and Nation," No. 263, *The Methodist Hymnal.*

RESOURCE MATERIALS

Education and the Disadvantaged American, 1962, National Education Association, 1201 16th Street, N. W., Washington 36, D. C. 35 cents.

Education and Training: Key to Development of Human Resources. Supt. of Documents, U.S. Government Printing Office, Washington, D. C. 20402. 40 cents.

"Give Slum Children a Chance: A Radical Proposal" by Charles Silberman, in **Harper's** magazine, May 1964. Harper's, 49 East 33rd Street, New York, New York 10016. 60 cents.

"I Remember Children" by Sharon Flynn in **The Methodist Woman**, January 1966. Service Center, 7820 Reading Road, Cincinnati, Ohio 45237.

New Opportunities for Depressed Areas by John D. Pomfret, Public Affairs Pamphlets, 381 Park Avenue South, New York, New York 10016. 25 cents.

Slums and Suburbs by James B. Conant, New American Library, 501 Madison Avenue, New York, New York 10012. 60 cents.

The Culturally Deprived Child by Frank Riessman, 1962, Harper & Row, Publishers, 49 East 33rd Street, New York, New York 10016. $3.95.

"Education in America" in **Saturday Review** magazine, 25 West 45th Street, New York, New York. 25 cents. (Contains several excellent articles on Project Headstart.)

TO CREATE

ORDER THE FOLLOWING FROM THE SERVICE CENTER
7820 READING ROAD, CINCINNATI, OHIO 45237

The Christian Case Against Poverty. By Dr. Henry Clark. (AY) 75 cents.

Poverty on a Small Planet: A Christian Looks at Living Standards. (MC) 95 cents.

MUST. Folder introducing Metropolitan-Urban Service Training Project. Free.

Metropolitan-Urban Service Training. A prospectus of the program. 16 pages. Free.

One Fifth of the Nation. A Fact and Action Guide. By Elma Greenwood. (NC) 50 cents.

ABOUT THE AUTHOR

Miss Sharon Flynn is originally from Rushford, New York, where she was active in The Methodist Church as church school teacher and conference president of MYF. She was graduated from State Universtiy College at Genesee, New York, with a B.S. in Elementary Education. While attending school she was state president of the Methodist Student Movement and involved with committees of the National Student Christian Federation.

This summer Miss Flynn was head teacher in the Operation Headstart program at Mt. Morris Presbyterian Church in New York City. She has had previous experience in teaching young children as a summer worker in both rural and inner city parishes. She has also taught first graders in Poughkeepsie, New York. She has been involved in the civil rights movement and participated in the march from Selma to Montgomery last spring.

She has done graduate work in sociology at Queens College and at the New School for Social Research in New York City. Currently, she is studying at Bank Street College of Education in the field of early childhood education. Miss Flynn worked as an editorial assistant with the Joint Commission on Education and Cultivation of the Board of Missions of The Methodist Church until February, 1966, when she resumed full-time teaching in the Operation Headstart program.

What It Feels Like to Be Negro in White America

MRS. P. Y. PATTERSON
AND
MRS. G. M. RICCIARDI

PURPOSE: To help develop new insights, new understandings, and new avenues of communication.

PRE-PROGRAM PLANNING:

(This program has been particularly planned so that white women might look at what some Negro writers of today are saying. However, the program is also intended to help other women, including Negro women, receive similar insights. It should be understood that the pronoun "we" used below refers to white women.)

As we hear what the Negro himself has written, perhaps we can begin to understand his search for identity, his struggle for freedom and dignity, and his concept of his role in society both in the past and now.

This program should help women examine some of their more stereotyped ideas about the Negro, and, perhaps, about other minority groups. As understanding of the Negro's life in a white-oriented culture grows, it is hoped that communication will begin to cross racial barriers that may have existed because of unfamiliarity, lack of knowledge, distrust, or even fear. As communication grows, it can lead to fellowship and Christian community. It is hoped that this program will lead from knowledge to understanding to communication to community.

PROGRAM SETTING: The women listening to the program should be sitting in a relaxed grouping—a semicircle, perhaps. It is hoped people will listen to the words and take little, if any, notice of the surroundings, themselves, and each other. To one side should be the program leader, perhaps with a lectern and small light. In the center facing the group should be a table with a small light directed down on the material on the table. The two readers will be seated here. The room should be dim so that light

TO CREATE

is played only on the material being read, and little, if any notice is taken of the readers themselves. It is suggested that for maximum impact only two readers, as indicated, present the program.

FIRST READER: Perhaps few of us have ever had the opportunity of knowing a Negro as a person. Literary works by Negroes can give us this opportunity as no other medium can. Through such literary works the white man has an unparalleled opportunity to see himself as others see him. It is an image we might prefer to turn away from, but it carries with it an undisguised challenge. Can we look squarely at this image, try to understand it, ask ourselves, "Do we deserve it" and then do what we can to repair it?

Most authors agree that they write out of their own experience. Nearly every Negro writer, though he may have quite a variety of subjects he hopes to encompass during his career, feels the need to write about the problem of race. This is *his* experience. This has been the problem of his life.

We want to try to share in the meaning of what it feels like to be "black" in "white America." This is the essence of the following selections. It is powerful, gripping material.

Hopefully, this will only be the beginning of an experience in understanding. We need to see what we look like to many Negroes. We need to put ourselves in another's shoes to understand and appreciate the revolution we're living through. And we hope you will read further, for yourselves, some of the books referred to here.

SECOND READER: Historian Louis Lomax, in his book *The Negro Revolt* (Harper & Row, Publishers, Incorporated), examines the three-hundred-year-old struggle of the American Negro for equal opportunity, equal recognition, and full freedom as a citizen. Mr. Lomax turns a critical eye on the usual presentation of American history when he writes:

"One of the great sins of general American history is that it omits the heroic deeds of white and Negro "officials" of the Underground Railroad [during the Civil War] . . . [These people] realized that the real enemy of freedom is within, not without, our country. . . . The white child never reads of these patriots, and their contribution to our tradition of freedom is omitted. As a result the Negro sit-ins and freedom riders look like Topsy; it is as if they 'jest growed,' whereas they are but another in the long line of courageous Americans who clanged freedom's bells while others would mute them."

Drawing on his experience as a journalist, author Lomax details incidents which provide a background for this "revolt":

" 'Lord, child,' a Mississippi woman once said to me, 'we colored people ain't nothing but a bundle of resentments and sufferings going somewhere to explode.'

"The explosion—and no one would have taken it for that—came on December 1, 1955, the day Mrs. Rosa Parks boarded the . . . bus in Montgomery, Alabama. And the Negro revolt is properly dated from the moment Mrs. Parks said 'No' to the bus driver's demand that she get up and let a white man have her seat.

"There have been scores of attempts to discover why Mrs. Parks refused to move. . . . The truth is that Mrs. Parks was a part of the deepening mood of despair and disillusionment that gripped the American Negro after World War II. She had been an official in the Montgomery NAACP; Mrs. Parks was an alert woman, a dedicated Negro, and fully aware of the continuing injustices Negroes all over the nation were enduring. The only way to account for Mrs. Parks is to say she was a part of the times; that, at long last, her cup ran over.

. . . .

[The following Monday the bus] boycott was on. So was the Negro revolt."

TO CREATE

FIRST READER: Novelist John Oliver Killens, in an article entitled "Explanation of the Black Psyche," which appeared in the *New York Times Magazine*,* writes from the inside looking out and says that:

"In order to justify slavery in a courageous new world which was spouting slogans of freedom and equality and brotherhood, the enslavers, through their propagandists, had to create the fiction that the enslaved people were subhuman and undeserving of human rights and sympathies. The first job was to convince the outside world of [their inferiority]. The second job was to convince the American people. And the third job, which was the cruelest hoax of all, was to convince the slaves themselves that they deserved to be slaves . . . the effects of [their success] remain with us."

But Killens is more hopeful as he later says:

"You look upon these times as the Atomic Age, the Space Age, the Cold War Era. But I believe that when the history of these times is written, . . . the great significance will be that this was the century when most of mankind achieved freedom and human dignity. For me, this is the Freedom Century.

.   .   .   .

"The Negro loves America enough to criticize her fundamentally . . . We are becoming prouder and prouder of our heritage in America and Africa . . . Yes, we black people stand ready, eager, willing and able to make our contribution to the culture of the world. Our dialogue will not be protest but *affirmation* of the human dignity of all people everywhere."

SECOND READER: *Native Son* ** is Richard Wright's story of a Negro boy's oppressed life in a Chicago slum—a

---

* © 1964 by The New York Times Company. Reprinted by permission. Reprinted from **Youngblood,** © 1954, by John O. Killens and used by permission of his publisher, Trident Press.

** Harper & Row, Publishers, Incorporated. Used by permission.

TO CREATE

life Wright knew from his own experience. Here he reminds us that:

"If only ten or twenty Negroes had been put into slavery, we could call it injustice, but there were hundreds of thousands of them throughout the country. If this state of affairs had lasted for two or three years, we could say that it was unjust; but it lasted for more than two hundred years. Injustice which lasts for three long centuries and which exists among millions of people over thousands of square miles of territory, is injustice no longer; it is an accomplished fact of life . . ."

FIRST READER: Before his murder, Mississippi-born Medgar Evers, the field secretary for the National Association for the Advancement of Colored People, was interviewed for an article which appeared in *Ebony* magazine entitled "Why I Live in Mississippi."* Evers said, in part:

"[I want freedom for my kids] . . . right here in Mississippi. And as long as God gives me strength to work and try to make things real for my children, I'm going to work for it—even if it means making the ultimate sacrifice . . .

". . . this is home [to me]. Mississippi is a part of the United States. And whether the whites like it or not, I don't plan to live here as a parasite. The things I don't like I will try to change, and in the long run, I hope to make a positive contribution to the overall productivity of the South . . .

"As a kid in Decatur, Mississippi, . . . [I grew up next door to a white playmate] who practically lived at my house . . . Then, one day, my friend stopped coming by. In a little while, he began to get nasty. Finally, out in the street with a group of his friends, he called me 'nigger.' The split had come. The lines were drawn, black on one side and white on the other. I guess at that

---
* Used by permission.

moment I realized my status in Mississippi. I have lived with it ever since. . . ."

SECOND READER: James Baldwin's writing epitomizes in some respects the head-on clash between black and white in American society. Considered a "fire-brand" novelist-essayist, Mr. Baldwin is a keen analyst of the current racial revolution in the United States. He is regarded by critics as the most soul-stirring talent to explode on the nation's contemporary literary scene.

His series of essays *The Fire Next Time** tells of the gradual realization of what it meant to him as a fourteen-year-old from Harlem to find himself a black man in a white man's world. He writes:

". . . School began to reveal itself . . . as a child's game that one could not win, and boys dropped out of school and went to work. My father wanted me to do the same. I refused, even though I no longer had any illusions about what an education could do for me; I had already encountered too many college graduate handymen.

. . . .

". . . one did not have to be very bright to realize how little one could do to change one's situation; one did not have to be abnormally sensitive to be worn down to a cutting edge by the incessant and gratuitous humiliation and danger one encountered every working day . . .

. . . .

"One would never defeat one's circumstances by working and saving one's pennies; one would never, by working, acquire that many pennies, and, besides, the social treatment accorded even the most successful Negroes proved that one needed, in order to be free, something more than a bank account . . . Neither civilized reason nor Christian love would cause white people to treat you as they presumably wanted to be treated; . . .

. . . .

---

* The Dial Press Inc. All quotes used by permission.

"... Yes, it does indeed mean something—something unspeakable—to be born, in a white country, an Anglo-Teutonic, antisexual country, black. You very soon, without knowing it, give up all hope of communion. Black people, mainly, look down or look up but do not look at each other, not at you, and white people, mainly, look away. And the universe is simply a sounding drum; there is no way, no way whatever, so it seemed then and has sometimes seemed since, to get through a life, to love your wife and children, or your friends, or your mother and father, or to be loved. The universe, which is not merely the stars and the moon and the planets, flowers, grass, and trees, but *other people*, has evolved no terms for your existence, has made no room for you, and if love will not swing wide the gates, no other power will or can. And if one despairs—as who has not?—of human love, God's love alone is left. But God—and I felt this even then, so long ago, on that tremendous floor, unwillingly—is white. And if His love was so great, and if He loved all His children, why were we, the blacks, cast down so far? Why? . . ."

Baldwin, too, is hopeful for the future as he says: "I am very much concerned that American Negroes achieve their freedom here in the United States. But I am also concerned for their dignity, for the health of their souls, and must oppose any attempt that Negroes may make to do to others what has been done to them . . . *Whoever debases others is debasing himself.* . . .

. . . .

"... I know that people can be better than they are. We are capable of bearing a great burden, once we discover that the burden is reality and arrive where reality is. Anyway, the point here is that we are living in an age of revolution, whether we will or no, and that America is the only Western nation with both power and, as I hope to suggest, the experience that may help to make these revolutions real and minimize the human damage. . . ."

Again, in another series of essays, *Nobody Knows My Name*,* James Baldwin voices the dispirited cry of all Negroes seeking recognition in our society as he says:

"Northerners indulge in an extremely dangerous luxury. They seem to feel that because they fought on the right side during the Civil War and won, they have earned the right merely to deplore what is going on in the South, without taking any responsibility for it and that they can ignore what is happening in Northern cities because what is happening in Little Rock and Birmingham is worse. Well, in the first place, it is not possible for anyone who has not endured both to know which is 'worse.' I know Negroes who prefer the South and white Southerners, because 'At least there, you haven't got to play any guessing games!'

.   .   .   .

"[The Northerner] never sees Negroes. Southerners see them all the time. Northerners never think about them whereas Southerners are never really thinking of anything else. Negroes are, therefore, ignored in the North and under surveillance in the South, and suffer hideously in both places. Neither the Southerner nor the Northerner is able to look on the Negro simply as a man. . . ."

FIRST READER: Langston Hughes has long been one of the most effective spokesmen for the American Negro. In a short and poignant poem, he visualizes a small Negro girl who grew up in the South but who has moved north. One day at a carnival she sees a merry-go-round and wants a ride, but remembering the color lines, she does not know if or where she can ride. This is what she says:

> Where is the Jim Crow section
> On this merry-go-round,
> Mister, cause I want to ride?

---

* The Dial Press Inc. Used by permission.

TO CREATE

> Down South where I come from
> White and colored
> Can't sit side by side.
> Down South on the train
> There's a Jim Crow car.
> On the bus we're put in the back—
> But there ain't no back
> To a merry-go-round!
> Where's the horse
> For a kid that's black?*

SECOND READER: In 1954 the Supreme Court declared segregation in public schools unconstitutional—the first major breakthrough in civil rights since the Emancipation Proclamation. But it was not until September 3, 1957, that nine Negro students registered at Central High School, Little Rock, Arkansas—the first of their race to do so. "The Battle of Little Rock" was a headline in newspapers around the world as National Guardsmen were called out and surrounded the school. Mrs. Daisy Bates, Arkansas President of the National Association for the Advancement of Colored People, writes vividly of those days in her book, *The Long Shadow of Little Rock*.**

Mrs. Bates was a close friend of the nine youngsters. They visited in her home; she talked with and listened to them both before and after the events of that September day. Elizabeth Eckford, one of the "embattled nine," as Mrs. Bates calls them, tells of her experience:

"That night I was so excited I couldn't sleep. The next morning I was the first one up. While I was pressing my black and white dress—I had made it to wear on the first day of school—my little brother turned on the

---
* "Merry-Go-Round," copyright, 1942 by Langston Hughes. Reprinted from *Shakespeare in Harlem* by Langston Hughes, by permission of Alfred A. Knopf, Inc.

** *The Long Shadow of Little Rock* by Daisy Bates, David McKay Company, Inc., New York, 1962. Used by permission.

TO CREATE

TV set. They started telling about a large crowd gathered at the school. The man on TV said he wondered if we were going to show up that morning. Mother called from the kitchen, where she was fixing breakfast, 'Turn that TV off!' She was so upset and worried. I wanted to comfort her, so I said, 'Mother, don't worry.'

"Dad was walking back and forth, from room to room, with a sad expression. He was chewing on his pipe and he had a cigar in his hand, but he didn't light either one. It would have been funny, only he was so nervous.

"Before I left home Mother called us into the living room. She said we should have a word of prayer. Then I caught the bus and got off a block from the school. I saw a large crowd of people standing across the street from the soldiers guarding Central. As I walked on, the crowd suddenly got very quiet. Superintendent Blossom had told us to enter by the front door. . . . I walked across the street conscious of the crowd that stood there, but they moved away from me.

"For a moment all I could hear was the shuffling of their feet. Then someone shouted, 'Here she comes, get ready!' I moved away from the crowd . . . and into the street. If the mob came at me I could then cross back over so the guards could protect me.

"The crowd moved in closer and then began to follow me, calling me names. I still wasn't afraid. Just a little bit nervous. Then my knees started to shake all of a sudden and I wondered whether I could make it to the center entrance a block away. It was the longest block I ever walked in my whole life.

"Even so, I still wasn't too scared because all the time I kept thinking that the guards would protect me.

"When I got right in front of the school, I went up to a guard . . . He just looked straight ahead and didn't move to let me pass him. I didn't know what to do. Then I looked and saw that the path leading to the front entrance was a little further ahead. So I walked until I

TO CREATE

was right in front of the path to the front door.

"I stood looking at the school—it looked so big! Just then the guards let some white students go through.

"The crowd was quiet. I guess they were waiting to see what was going to happen. When I was able to steady my knees, I walked up to the guard who had let the white students past him. He too didn't move. When I tried to squeeze past him, he raised his bayonet and then the other guards closed in and they raised their bayonets.

"They glared at me with a mean look and I was very frightened and didn't know what to do. I turned around and the crowd came toward me.

"They moved closer and closer. Somebody started yelling, 'Lynch her! Lynch her!'

"I tried to see a friendly face somewhere in the mob —someone who maybe would help. I looked into the face of an old woman and it seemed a kind face, but when I looked at her again, she spat on me.

"They came closer, shouting, 'No nigger bitch is going to get in our school. Get out of here!'

"I turned back to the guards but their faces told me I wouldn't get help from them. Then I looked down the block and saw a bench at the bus stop. I thought, 'If I can only get there I will be safe.' I don't know why the bench seemed a safe place to me, but I started walking toward it. I tried to close my mind to what they were shouting, and kept saying to myself, 'If I can only make it to the bench I will be safe.'

"When I finally got there, I don't think I could have gone another step. I sat down and the mob crowded up and began shouting all over again. Someone hollered, 'Drag her over to this tree! Let's take care of the nigger.' Just then a white man sat down beside me, put his arm around me and patted my shoulder. He raised my chin and said, 'Don't let them see you cry.'

"Then, a white lady—she was very nice—she came over to me on the bench. She spoke to me but I don't re-

TO CREATE

member now what she said. She put me on the bus and sat next to me. She asked me my name and tried to talk to me but I don't think I answered. I can't remember much about the bus ride, but the next thing I remember I was standing in front of the School for the Blind, where Mother works.

"I thought, 'Maybe she isn't here. But she has to be here!' So I ran upstairs and I think some teachers tried to talk to me, but I kept running until I reached Mother's classroom.

"Mother was standing at the window with her head bowed, but she must have sensed I was there because she turned around. She looked as if she had been crying, and I wanted to tell her I was all right. But I couldn't speak. She put her arms around me and I cried."

FIRST READER: The program to which you have been listening is a shortened and adapted version of one which was put together by a circle in Leonia, New Jersey. The members of the Leonia group found much personal challenge and involvement in reading through many books and articles by Negro writers and in selecting the quotations which seemed to speak most clearly.

Now we must turn to our own group, where the question might be, "What do I myself feel about this program? Have I gained any insights from hearing the statements which were made today?" More specifically, each one of us might ask herself:

What are some of the images the Negro has of himself and of the white man?

Do I see with new eyes some aspects of those human beings who are Negroes, and what have I learned from this program I did not know before?

What aspect of the program most impressed me?

How can our group play a part in communication, understanding, and Christian fellowship and community among all people, and what does my role need to be?

TO CREATE

Perhaps it would be good for us to take time now to share our thoughts on these questions with each other. (FIRST READER *might here ask specific members to share their thoughts on some of the above questions. Probably all members should be encouraged to make some contribution to the discussion.*)

REFERENCES APPEARING IN PROGRAM

The Negro Revolt, Louis Lomax. New American Library (paperback), 75 cents.

"Exploration of the Black Psyche," John Oliver Killens. **New York Times Magazine,** June 7, 1964. Also in **Youngblood,** Trident Press, 1954.

Native Son, Richard Wright. New American Library (paperback), 75 cents.

"Why I Live in Mississippi," Medgar Evers. **Ebony** magazine, 18:143-8, Sept. 1963.

The Fire Next Time, James Baldwin. Dell (paperback), 50 cents.

Notes of a Native Son, James Baldwin. Bantam Books (paperback), 60 cents.

Nobody Knows My Name, James Baldwin. Dell (paperback), 50 cents.

"Merry-Go-Round," Langston Hughes. In **Shakespeare in Harlem,** Alfred A. Knopf, 1942.

The Long Shadow of Little Rock, by Daisy Bates. McKay, $5.50.

Other books of interest:

Raisin in the Sun, Lorraine Hansberry. New American Library (paperback), 60 cents.

Manchild in the Promised Land, Claude Brown. Macmillan, $6.95.

Invisible Man, Ralph Ellison. New American Library (paperback), 95 cents.

Nigger, Dick Gregory and R. Lipsyte. Pocket Books (paperback), 75 cents.

Yes I Can, Sammy Davis, Jr. Farrar, Straus & Giroux, $6.95.

Americans All, a mimeographed bibliography listing recommended books concerned with the problem of minorities (for kindergarten through adult). Free. Write to: Hilda Lee Dail, Room 1366, 475 Riverside Drive, New York, N. Y. 10027.

ORDER THE FOLLOWING FROM THE SERVICE CENTER
7820 READING ROAD, CINCINNATI, OHIO 45237

Sense and Nonsense About Race. By Ethel J. Alpenfels. An anthropologist's answer to questions asked frequently about race and racial differences. Second revision. 75 cents.

Youth Guide on Races and Reconciliation. By Newell S. Booth, Jr. Detailed plans for programs and action projects using **Seeking to Be Christian in Race Relations, Sense and Nonsense About Race, What Can We Do?, Must Walls Divide?** and other resources. 75 cents. (See catalog for booklets listed above.)

Two Decades. Booklet giving background for the revised Charter on Racial Policies. 25 cents.

A Charter of Racial Policies. Leaflet on action adopted by the General Conference of The Methodist Church on May 8, 1964, for implementation by its members and churches. 5 cents each; 6 for 25 cents.

A Charter of Racial Policies. Poster, 20 x 28½ inches, 25 cents. Small, 11 x 16 inches, 6 for 25 cents.

Twentieth Century Americans of Negro Lineage Pictomap. By Louise E. Jefferson. Resource sheet by James H. Robinson. Photos of some outstanding contemporary Negroes and drawings in color showing highlights of Negro vocational achievement are superimposed on an outline of the United States. Resource sheet gives information and suggestions for use. Small, 13 x 9¾ inches, 75 cents a dozen. Wall size, 40 x 30 inches, folded $1.50; rolled $2.00.

ORDER THE FOLLOWING FROM THE WRIGHT STUDIO
5264 BROOKVILLE ROAD, INDIANAPOLIS, INDIANA 46219

Freedom Napkin. Decorated with Liberty's torch and challenging quotations. 50 for 80 cents.

Race Puzzlemat. Placemat decorated with some optical illusions that suggest that many beliefs about race are also illusions. 20 for 75 cents.

Race Creative Uses. Interpretation of accessories along with many helpful ideas for their use. 10 cents.

to Participate...

in dialogue
with other women
about the dilemmas of a
diverse society

In Dialogue With Women of Southeast Asia

HELEN LOOMIS

PURPOSE: To discover some of the dilemmas of a diverse society, and to understand how some of the dilemmas of women in other countries are similar to our own.

PRE-PROGRAM PLANNING:

These are the true experiences of a missionary who has worked for many years in China and Southeast Asia. It is suggested that this might be presented as a TV interview with two people taking part: Missionary and Commentator

There are numerous local and national radio and television programs using this basic format which may serve as models. Develop one best suited to your own group. Following the interview there could be audience participation with questions directed to the missionary. Some suggested questions will be found listed at the end of the program.

You can make this an elaborate program or a very simple one. If you are in a location where there are foreign students, or persons having costumes, you may be able to arrange to have the actions of each scene pantomimed in the background while the Commentator and Missionary are talking.

Several episodes contain the basis for excellent meditational thoughts. Perhaps one of your group might take the program and write a litany which would incorporate the various concepts reflected here. This would serve as a fitting conclusion to the program. If possible—where there are foreign students or visitors available—you might want to ask some of these folks to pray in their own language. If this is done, it might be wise to have the prayer in English beforehand and made available for the group so they can understand the contents of each prayer.

ACTION THAT COULD GROW OUT OF THE PROGRAM:

There are many illiterates in the United States. Are any of

them in your community? Discover ways your group might help in such a program: contact your local Board of Education, or social agencies for information.

Are there small, rural church groups in your area which need help with their women's groups? Are there any ways you can help?

If you are in a rural area, perhaps there is some assistance you can offer through the County Home Demonstration Agent.

COMMENTATOR: Methodist circuit riders of old had nothing on some of today's workers in the church around the world. Take Southeast Asia as an example. Here is a complex society made up of numerous ethnic and religious backgrounds—a series of small, struggling nations made up of islands and peninsulas in the Indian Ocean and the South China Sea.

Let us visit these lands with a missionary who has been island-hopping for a decade. Like many of her fellow missionaries she has traveled into remote regions visiting small villages to work with Christian women isolated from the rest of the world. Assigned to the former Southeast Asia Central Conference (of The Methodist Church) she made regular visits of from six weeks to four months into Burma, Sumatra, Sarawak, Malaya, and Singapore.

Women around the world have ideas, longings, problems, and dreams which they share and discuss with other women—their uniqueness lies only in their location and their varied cultural backgrounds. By looking through the eyes of this American missionary, perhaps we can "see" these women as women rather than seeing them as Chinese, Ibans, Bataks, or Tamils. Suppose we ask our missionary friend to conduct us on this "armchair visit."

MISSIONARY: This is a story of some beginnings. It is also about some results of those beginnings. Sometimes God can speak more clearly and more truly through some of his less privileged and less sophisticated sons and daughters than through those whom the world calls great. Let me tell you about an example we found in Malaysia.

(*Pause to allow scene to be set or just to make the break between this introduction and the story that follows.*)

It was impossible to tell where the entrance to the little church was. The small building was badly in need of paint and the Chinese characters and English words over the door which should have read *Methodist Church* were only faint shadows on the weather-beaten frame. I wondered just how we could expect any respect for Christianity with churches looking like this. My Chinese colleague and I went up the well worn path at the side, but stopped short as we came to the fence.

"This can't be the way in," I said. "Look, the path goes right through the yard of this Moslem family. You know the unwritten law here in Malaysia rules out our teaching Christianity to Moslems. How can we possibly go through their very yard to get into our church?"

"There is no other way to get into the building," my friend said, but she looked as troubled as I did as we quickly crossed the yard and went in the back door of the church. Although it was quite run-down, there was evidence that someone had been trying to keep the place clean. Inside we found six or seven older Chinese women waiting for us. They were all dressed in the usual wide-legged black trousers, some wearing blue, some white jackets. Most of the younger people had moved away after the war. In this small village, as in so many others, the post-war depression had lingered for a number of years.

Before the meeting, the smallest woman there volunteered to read the Bible. Only after the worship service began did we discover that her "reading" was really just memorization of John 3:16 which she had once learned. We also discovered that not one of the women knew a hymn, not even the Doxology. And worse yet, no one seemed to know any of the Lord's Prayer.

Though illiterate, these were business women, most of whom kept close track of their family's money. Our "reader" was even the church treasurer. They seemed quite learned in the ways of the world, but pitifully ignorant of the things of God.

We found many small churches in this same condition. These women needed help—help of a special sort that would make them aware of what the church could mean to them and how much they could mean to the church. How we needed someone who could speak the various Chinese dialects, who could meet with these people and help them! As we returned the three hundred miles to Kuala Lumpur that night, we discussed this problem. There seemed no answer, for we had neither the person nor the money to begin any such work. (*Slight pause.*)

A letter from New York changed all that. We could hardly believe it. The letter from the Board of Missions said, "Now we can include your area as one to benefit from gifts. We have received more money than we expected from the Week of Prayer and Self-Denial. Do you have a plan for training women leaders in the local church? If so, send it to us. If it is a workable plan, we shall be glad to help you put it into operation since these funds are now available."

My Chinese friend spoke first. "It seems like an answer to our prayers. But what about a plan? What about a worker? We have a need, but we haven't gotten as far as a plan yet."

Finally I said, "We've just got to work out a plan. Let's sit down and see if we can't work out something together. We will need a full-time worker . . . ," I began and then looked at my friend. "What about you? You used to work in the church—would you go back into full-time work?"

She had been a church worker for more than twenty years, all during the Japanese occupation of her country.

TO PARTICIPATE

To support her family she had to leave her low-paying church job and take a teaching position in a government school. I knew she had always wanted to go back into full-time church work; because of her interest she had continued working with church women. Now she was our conference president helping me as we visited these groups. I didn't have to ask her twice, for she said, "You know I've always wanted to go back into church work. I'm sure I could manage it now that the children are grown. Yes, if we can work out an acceptable plan, I'll be available for the job."

That settled it. Our plan was to take a program of renewal of Christian purpose and leadership training as well as to bring some knowledge of better living methods to these women in remote areas. Their pattern of living restricted them to the care of children and the home—they seldom got out. To be most workable, our plan would have to allow for home visitation if we expected to reach the women who really needed our help.

Two of us couldn't possibly cover all the groups needing help. We agreed that there were larger, more organized city societies whose members we could call on for assistance as volunteers. Such a plan would really serve two purposes: help these larger groups gain a broader vision of their mission, and give them leadership training.

Our plan was accepted and we began. During the first year we were able to visit every Chinese-speaking Woman's Society of Christian Service in the area, and that area included Malaysia, Sarawak, North Borneo, Malaya, Burma and Sumatra.

Besides leadership training we were able to get district and even some subdistrict organizations established.

COMMENTATOR: I can easily see how you could visit local societies, but do you mean to say that these women, most of whom are quite restricted to their homes, were interested in or able to participate in any kind of district or subdistrict program?

MISSIONARY: Let me tell you of an incident and you'll have your answer. It took place at a subdistrict meeting. After most of the women had gone, one tiny woman remained, and she came up to us with tears in her eyes and said, "Can't you send us someone to teach us to read? I want all the women of my society to know the things we have been learning today. But how can I take it all back to them? I cannot read or write. No one in our church can read or write."

As she continued to talk I recalled what someone had told me about this little lady when she arrived at the meeting earlier in the day. We were meeting in a small city down the Rejang River from Sibu, Sarawak. To get there she had cycled for several miles, part of the way through the rubber gardens, then left her cycle with a friend and walked a mile or so to the river. There she had taken a launch to the city where we were meeting and had to walk at least another mile from the river to get to the church!

COMMENTATOR (*interrupting*): You mean to say that she was so interested in attending the Woman's Society she would travel all that distance? I certainly can't imagine women in this country even going to half that trouble to attend a meeting, no matter if it were their local society or the subdistrict. Yes, I can see that these women are eager to learn, but tell us, were you able to help this woman?

MISSIONARY: I'm sure you know that literacy remains one of the most urgent problems in the world today. Even in the United States there are many who cannot read or write. Sometimes it is difficult for us in America to realize how it feels *not* to be able to read or write.

TO PARTICIPATE

In Southeast Asia it is a tremendous problem. How could we expect to have any programs used in local Woman's Societies if no one could read or write? Some illiterate women were able to remember as many as four or five programs to take back to their local group. But this woman was suddenly overwhelmed with her own and her group's very real need for literacy. We wondered how many others who had attended the meeting were just like her, but hadn't had the courage to come to us with their problem.

Our work was only a beginning. We did not have anyone trained, nor money for a literacy project. We knew others shared this same concern, and realized that their concern had grown during the years—by then it was almost ten—since we first put our plan into action to help them understand their church and recognize what the extent of their Christian responsibility ought to be.

This was like a Macedonian call: "Can't you send us someone to teach us to read?" Even though Sibu Theological School was making plans to send a graduate student with a major concern for literacy out into the villages, this would only touch a small part of the problem. The Methodist Church has now begun to respond to this need by placing a major emphasis on literacy and literature, by assigning special persons to survey the problem and discover how the church may become more involved in solving it.

COMMENTATOR: I should think it would be extremely difficult to try to establish any Christian education programs when so many people are illiterate. This seems like something we all ought to be more concerned about. It's hard for us to realize that many people don't have the wonderful opportunities we have for learning and for Christian fellowship. We hear that, in spite of our technological advances, there is still a tremendous gap between what we have and what most other people have.

TO PARTICIPATE

MISSIONARY: That reminds me of another story. It's about some Iban women who wondered about that "gap," as you call it.

COMMENTATOR: Iban women? Those are the people who live in Sarawak, North Borneo, aren't they?

MISSIONARY: Suppose we visit them. The incident I recall happened at a women's meeting some years ago. The questioner interrupted the meeting to ask, "Do you think we Iban women will ever catch up with the other women of the world?" I almost missed the importance of the question as the bright young woman spoke. I was so busy staring at her that I couldn't concentrate on what she said. Really, you can hardly imagine the sight: between her open lips gleamed four brightly colored teeth —one red, one blue, one yellow, and one green! And each of them was edged with gold! I've seen gold teeth before but never multi-colored teeth. However, the question this young woman asked was as startling as her appearance. I was puzzled as to how she had come to know about the "other women of the world." Here we were in the jungles of Sarawak, seemingly far removed from the rest of the world. Then I noticed that she was wearing Western-style clothes while all the other women at the meeting were dressed in the usual Indonesian sarong and kabaya (blouse). Ordinarily, these Iban women omit a blouse and wear only a twenty-two inch sarong skirt when in their homes or traveling up and down the river, which is like "Main Street" to them. Occasionally they may wear a hat, a large straw one for protection from the sun. For special times like the meeting, the women wore blouses. In fact, they had all come in their "traveling clothes" with a small bundle hung on poles slung over their shoulders. Just before entering the meeting they had stopped, untied their bundles, put on their blouses and long sarongs. But the young woman who had asked the question was different: she wore a Western-style dress, had her hair cut short . . . and she asked questions!

I was completely at a loss to answer her. What answer could I give? There flashed through my mind the picture of my many visits to Iban homes—those long wooden buildings, with thatched roofs, set on stilts, built along the banks of the river. An entire "clan" of anywhere from fifteen to fifty families sometimes live in one long house. Partitions give each family a small cubicle all under one roof. This is home to Iban women, and they spend their entire lives in isolation there.

Within these compact and often congested quarters they carry on their daily tasks: caring for children, cooking over small smoky fires, grinding flour, weaving material for their brightly colored sarongs, doing all their household jobs by the most primitive methods. Sometimes they may help with the planting, tending, or harvesting of rice while their husbands fish, collect rubber, or work at lumbering. Rarely does a woman ever leave this communal setting except on those occasions when she may travel to a nearby Chinese trading village. If she is ill enough, she may travel down the river to Kapit and Christ Hospital.

Again the young woman's question stirred my mind: "Could these Iban women ever 'catch up'?"

Many Ibans are Christians. The first Ibans (thirty of them) were baptized in 1949. By 1963 there were between six and seven thousand Iban Methodists. They literally became Christians "one long house at a time"— an entire family "clan" accepting the new faith together.

Missionaries spurred agricultural development, encouraging primitive people to retain old skills while developing the potential of their oil, rubber and timber-rich land. The entire area had prospered because of this.

The young questioner became more insistent, "Can

we Iban women change? Will we ever catch up with the rest of the world?"

"It will take time and much work, but you can learn," I told her. Then I was interrupted by an older Iban woman who told us, "I have changed. In my old religion (these tribespeople were nearly all animists) we feared evil spirits. You know, like when birds fly over and make a certain noise, we thought it was an evil sign and we must stop planting or harvesting. But then we only got more hungry. When I became a Christian, I learned that God who made us and the birds, who made the seeds to grow and the harvest to come, our God is a loving God like a loving father. Now we do not have fear. Yes, we Ibans can change."

COMMENTATOR: Did they change? What happened when these women became Christians?

MISSIONARY: In a very few years, less than a decade, as many as one hundred and fifty Iban women representing organized local Woman's Societies of Christian Service attended the annual meeting of the Conference Society. If I hadn't known these women before, I never could have believed that they were the same I had once met on the day the young woman with multi-colored teeth asked questions!

At this conference they were dressed in colorful sarongs and blouses. Their participation was almost unbelievable. Only a year later they organized their own conference society and sent their president and two elected delegates to the quadrennial meeting of the Southeastern Asia Central Conference. At the close of that meeting they presented a beautifully woven prayer mat for the prayer chapel. As I listened to the women tell of their growing spiritual companionship with Christ and of their experience with other Iban women as they worked together in their church, I recalled the young woman and her question. It had taken time, and hard work, but Iban women were beginning to "catch up."

COMMENTATOR: It must be quite challenging to work in an area where people from so many racial backgrounds live. You've told us about the Chinese and now about the Ibans. I suppose you have some different problems, too, that arise because these are new nations.

MISSIONARY: Indeed we do. It is a real problem for some of these countries to weld into one nation people from so many racial and cultural backgrounds. On my way to a church conference one day I was traveling with my Chinese co-worker, and we stopped at a small restaurant for a meal. As we were eating, a Tamil pastor who had a church in that town came up to us. These people, who originally came from southern India, work on the rubber plantations, for the railroads, and in many factories. They have a separate language church. The pastor confronted me with the question, "When are you coming to our church with your leadership training program? I do not understand why you work so much with the Chinese churches and never come to us."

Actually I had visited several Tamil churches, but I had to admit that there was much yet to be done among that group. They had so many problems: most educated Tamils have gone to English schools and their children have entirely forgotten or never known their mother tongue, yet the churches used only Tamil. Some of the English-speaking Tamil women were helpful as we tried to cope with the problem. We began by using small teams of women to visit in the homes. But they were not used to this kind of activity. In India some of them had taken part in such programs, but this was Malaya. These women were faced with the problems of a rapidly changing social order—they were torn between the old and the new. They delighted in social occasions but would not come if we proposed a study group.

Finally we confronted them with a challenge by telling them that they were the only ones who could share the love of Christ with others in the rubber plantations or labor-lines where most of them lived and where their families worked. In the discussion that followed one of the older women finally said, "If America can send us missionaries, surely we can help our own people." That was the beginning. The programs were carried outside the city to other Tamil churches, and for a time we had a young Tamil girl who worked full time. Now she is married, and there is need for someone else to take over this work. But we are constantly faced with these many problems: language difficulties, cultural differences which do not leave women free or willing to assume a leadership role, as well as the divisions that these (language and culture or race) make among the community at large.

COMMENTATOR: Listening to you tell about these various groups with whom you have been working, I can see how these problems would sometimes appear almost insurmountable. Even here in the United States we can find homes where the parents speak a foreign language and the children are learning English in school. In many ways, I suppose that the problems you have to face are really not too different from the ones we could find in our own communities.

MISSIONARY: If we could only come to realize how very much alike our problems are, perhaps we could come to a closer understanding of one another. Take, for example, the Bataks. Only a hundred years or so ago the first missionary in Batakland was killed and eaten by the people, who were cannibals. But in a meeting with these women, we asked them where they found it most difficult to be a Christian, and one woman answered with this problem, which I'm sure you will find familiar in some details. She said, "I cannot read or write. My teen-age children go to school. They know more than I do. That is good. But they will not obey me. That is not good. Some teachers and some older students tell my children, 'Don't do what your mother and father tell you. Do what you please. Don't go to church, don't go to Sunday school or youth fellowship.' Now my children will have nothing to do with the church. What am I to do?"

Her question was echoed by the entire group, and so we discussed ways they might apply their Christian faith to their home problems. An unusual aspect of this was in neighbor relations, since Batak homes are all open and houses are close together so that everything said or done in one house is quite easily heard or seen from the next.

But this problem of what to do about their teen-age children topped the list. It seems to be universal, this rebellion of the young against the old—or against authority. We came up with some answers although no more solutions than you would. But through these discussions, the women did come to a new realization of their need to be Christian in their daily lives and that they could gain strength through prayer and seeking God's guidance. The Woman's Society is a lifesaver for these Batak women. It is there they go with their sorrows, problems, troubles. In sharing they learn together. As we closed our meeting one woman who had sat silent a long while spoke: "I never knew that is what it meant to be a Christian," she said. "Why hasn't someone told us this before—how we can have Christ live in our lives. You will have to tell us again and again so we will remember—we never knew before."

COMMENTATOR: Perhaps we take our education too much for granted. In our Woman's Society and Guild meetings we don't always face such everyday problems as these women seem to. Maybe there are many of us who could say, along with that Batak woman, "We never knew," yet we have so many more opportunities for coming to know than they. These women are a challenge to us to reflect more of Christ in our everyday lives.

QUESTIONS

1. In what ways are the problems of American and Southeast Asian women the same? Different?
2. How does your group—Woman's Society, Circle, or Wesleyan Service Guild—serve as a sounding board for the problems most often faced by its members? How do you find solutions in fellowship with other women?
3. Discuss ways in which your group could create dialogue out of dilemma.
4. How do you and your family express your Christianity? Discuss one of the women you heard about today in whose circumstances you would find it difficult to be a Christian.
5. How is Jesus' teaching, "Seek ye first the Kingdom of God" relevant today? What bearing does it have on how we spend our time?

RESOURCES

ORDER THE FOLLOWING FROM THE SERVICE CENTER
7820 READING ROAD, CINCINNATI, OHIO 45237

Free leaflets in the "Methodist Work in New Nations" series:
Burma
The Federation of Malaysia: Sarawak
Indonesia (Sumatra)
The Federation of Malaysia: States of Malaya and Singapore

Children on the Rim of East Asia. Free.

Who Are the Chinese in Dispersion? Color, pictures. 12 pages. Free.

Political Map of Southeast Asia. (Burma, Thailand, Malaya, Indonesia, Philippines) 40 x 30 inches. 75 cents.

TO PARTICIPATE

ORDER THE FOLLOWING FROM THE WRIGHT STUDIO
5264 BROOKVILLE ROAD, INDIANAPOLIS, INDIANA 46219

Cut-outs of Southern Asians. Twenty people of Southern Asia in full color costume printed back to back on ten cut-outs. $1.25 per set.

Friendship Bracelet. Metallic cord replica of band made for annual Indian friendship festival. Each 8 cents.

Friendship Ceremony. Use with bracelet for an impressive, meditative service of fellowship with Indian women. 10 cents.

ABOUT THE AUTHOR

Helen Loomis, born in New York State, has spent much of her life working in and for China. Originally a student of architecture at George Washington University, she decided that "building with people rather than stone, sand, and mortar" was more important and went on to receive an M.A. from Boston University's School of Religious Education.

In China she spent five years as administrative secretary to the chairman of the China National Christian Council. During this time she supervised Sunday schools and taught art appreciation. Back in the U.S., she was associated with many organizations to aid China, among them United China Relief, The American China Policy Association, and the China Information Service.

After working in hospital administration and on the editorial staff of the New York edition of *The Shanghai Evening Post and Mercury*, she traveled extensively in Southeast Asia teaching, editing, writing, and working with women's groups.

She is now in Korea where she is working with women.

to Encounter...

> God in the experiences
> of shared sorrow
> and joy
> with other women
> in the world

In Shared Sorrow | VIRGINIA LAW

PURPOSES: To consider how Christian faith can help one be victorious in the face of personal sorrow.

To share with all women our common sorrows as expressed in these varied circumstances of life.

NOTE TO PROGRAM COMMITTEE:

You may want to preface the presentation of this program with this information about the author.

Mrs. Burleigh (Virginia) Law is the widow of a missionary killed by Congolese rebels during the fighting of 1964. Out of the depth of her own experience she shares these incidents which have brought her to a better understanding of how we encounter God through shared experiences of sorrow. (See p. 31)

PRE-PROGRAM PLANNING:

Have one of the group read through the program before you meet. Then have her read it to the group in an informal situation —seated, group in a circle, casual arrangement. Or you may wish to let several people read, using the subtitles to give clues as to where breaks might be. As your group shares in these experiences —as Mrs. Law tells them—you will recall occasions in your own life experience when you learned these same lessons. Some may wish to share such experiences with the rest of the group.

Perhaps you will want to discover together answers to the following questions at the end of the program: (They may be assigned beforehand if this seems advisable.)

How do we allow God to work through our grief?

How does God help us give up self-pity?

Discuss the meanings of: Romans 5:3; 12:12. (You may want someone to prepare some background for this beforehand. Go to the Abingdon Bible Commentary, The Interpreter's Bible, or similar resource books to discover fuller meanings of these passages. Do not take the single verse, but seek to understand it in its fuller context.)

Have you ever reacted to a situation like Virginia Law did when she did not want to see her friend who had been divorced, gun, the older boy thought they were safe. Neither Marge nor I knew they had them until, as we sat sewing on her porch, we heard, "Bang! Bang! Bang!" followed by Congolese wildly yelling. We rushed out to the back yard to find bullets shooting off in all directions from the fire where they had been thrown while three little boys watched with glee from behind a palm tree. Again we all joined in laughing.

On and on it went for hours—recalling the serious, the funny, the naughty, the lovable Rickie as each of us had known him.

Suddenly it dawned upon me, "Why, we are sitting here laughing about Rickie when he's dead. How terrible!" I turned to Marge.

"Marge, I just don't see how you can talk so joyfully about Rickie."

Then Marge shared with me this incident which made a great difference in my life years later.

Immediately after Rickie's death she was crushed by such a loss. Rickie had been a brilliant child with great promise. They could not understand why he should be taken. I had heard how bravely Marge and Hugh had accepted it. Still their hearts wept and grieved. They were burdened by their sorrow.

In their home there were five other children. They did their very best to comfort their parents. Then one day Marge realized none of them ever mentioned Rickie in any way. When talking about some incident in which he had been a part, they just avoided his name. They acted as if they had forgotten him. This went on for weeks until one day again Rickie was left out of some story in which he had been such a big part. With sobs Marge asked, "Have you children forgotten Rickie so soon?"

Startled, all five children looked at Marge. They were shocked. For moments they sat, all five staring at her. Then the oldest, Kay, answered, "Why no, Mother. We remember Rickie all the time when we are alone. We just don't mention him here in the house for we don't want to see you cry."

Telling me of this Marge said, "I realized that we had to remember Rickie in joy and sorrow, and by God's grace it would be in joy."

Beginning then, at that dinner table, Marge encouraged the children to recall events in which Rickie had taken part. Once again he became a part of their family, bringing joy into their lives.

"Not a Pollyanna"

This is not a Pollyanna "Count your blessings." This is a realistic praising God for those lessons you learn in your sorrow, for a clearer understanding of the sufferings of others, for the ability to accept these sorrows, and for His Grace which holds you steady and supports your life in such times of strain.

Even though I carried my load of grief all day, fighting to keep back my tears, forcing a smile, at night I would fall exhausted on my bed. I tried to look up to God and say in all sincerity, "Father, I'm here. I can't do this alone. Take this load." Then, in a way unexplainable, the load would lift and rest, with a deep peace, would come. But what about tomorrow?

Tomorrow brings a new day, and I often found facing the "tomorrows" difficult. Not long after Burleigh's death, a friend who had been a widow for several years said to me, "I hate to tell you, Virginia, but the loneliness gets worse as time goes on."

Later, alone in my room, I cried, "Oh, Father in heaven, it can't get worse. I just couldn't stand it any worse. I'm taking now all I can possibly stand." Then, deep within my heart there came an answer. God was saying to me, "Virginia, don't worry about the 'tomorrows.' You don't need Wednesday's grace on Monday."

I lay and pondered. Unlike the Congolese woman carrying her dead child, I had hope. I could share in the loneliness of the widow and of my divorced friend. I could extend my friendship to them—as my friend had to me—to listen, to pray, and just to be nearby to help break that "alone" feeling. I had learned that one doesn't just "keep the chin up." I had to seek God's help on my knees—to encounter God personally. He didn't make my load lighter, but he did put "reinforcements under my bridges." I had seen how another mother's unselfish love had reconciled and healed both the forgiver and the forgiven. I found that work is no real answer unless it is "work that forces us to look out upon others." Guided by the words of the Apostle Paul and the experience of a missionary friend I discovered, as she had, that we had to remember our dead loved ones in joy or sorrow.

Yes, God does give strength through grace to meet each day's problems and suffering—but only one day at a time, and in such ways we can encounter Him.

RESOURCES

ORDER THE FOLLOWING FROM THE SERVICE CENTER
7820 READING ROAD, CINCINNATI, OHIO 45237

Free leaflets in the "Methodist Work in New Nations" series: **The Republic of Congo (Leopoldville).**

Picture Packets. Africa. Set of six 8 x 10-inch black and white glossy photos with caption sheet, title cards and suggestions for display. Sale each $1.50.

Spiritual Life Cultivation. Free.

Say a Prayer with Me before You Go. Leaflet which discusses the problem of how to pray with loved ones who may be dying, and how to face their loss. 3 cents each; 10 for 25 cents.

Who Would Valiant Be? A leaflet of comfort and inspiration to those in sorrow. 5 cents each; 25 for 40 cents.

Fellowship of Intercession Card. Free.

A record, interview about the death of Burleigh Law, **Modern Martyrdom,** was distributed to every Methodist pastor with his December 1965 issue of **The Methodist Story.** If your pastor does not have a copy, limited supplies are available from the Service Center. Free.

In Moments of Joy

HARRIET SEIBERT

PURPOSES: To experience joyous encounters with God in the varied circumstances of life.

To learn to reflect this joy with gratitude.

NOTE TO PROGRAM COMMITTEE:

Because of the unique personality of the author we have included a brief sketch of her life which should be used as part of the program itself—it may be read or told as seems most effective.

PRE-PROGRAM PLANNING:

This program is intended to be presented in the spirit of worship.

It is important to select a skilled leader who will encourage members of the group to participate. Perhaps each of the sections may be given to different women well in advance of the meeting so that they can become acquainted with the contents for the most effective presentation. This presentation may be as written or in their own words.

Each portion is intended to guide the group into reflection on their own personal experiences. A short period may be given following each presentation for sharing similar experiences of individual members.

Additional ideas and background for the second presentation may be found in copies of **The Methodist Woman** and **World Outlook.**

You may want to select your own hymns. Those used here are suggestions of appropriate themes.

Perhaps someone in the group is a soloist; it might be effective to have the suggested verses of "Still, Still with Thee" presented that way. In fact, you may find it more effective to have at least one verse of each of the hymns sung as solos, with the group joining in on the second or third verses.

The aim is for the group to leave the meeting with a feeling of joyous dedication.

TO ENCOUNTER

INTRODUCTION:

There are few who are able to express joy and hope in the face of adversity. But Harriet Seibert, whose experiences and ideas have been adapted for this program, reflects that "stability to face any problem" of which she speaks. Since she retired, Harriet has gradually lost her sight, despite several operations, yet she continues to "see" with those inner eyes of the spirit which God has given her.

Following her graduation from Barnard College and Columbia University, Miss Seibert's first professional position was as the Director of Christian Education at Christ Church, Methodist, New York City. She was on the staff there with Dr. Ralph W. Sockman for fifteen years.

During World War II she carried out some pioneer work as liaison person between the Women's Army Corps and local churches in Florida and Iowa. This work was jointly sponsored by the Woman's Division of The Methodist Church and the United Church Women. Later she worked in temporary housing areas in California and with students in Michigan.

For more than ten years she was on the staff of the Woman's Division of the Methodist Board of Missions as Secretary of Field Cultivation. Through these years she planned itinerations for missionaries, deaconesses and church visitors from overseas most effectively. Her dedication to this work and her spirit of service have been an inspiration to many.

JOYOUS ENCOUNTER WITH GOD IN THE EARLY DAWN AND THROUGH THE DAY

HYMN NO. 40, *The Methodist Hymnal*, "Still, Still With Thee"

(Have someone read or sing as a solo verses 1 and 3)

Blest indeed is the person who, in his early waking hours, has the certainty that God is with him as he enters had come were blind, or nearly so; he had much work to do and must get home quickly. He must tell them how beautiful the opening leaves on a grape vine were; these he had first seen when he came to my house just after receiving his sight. He must tell them of the range of color of the zinnias and dahlias in our garden, of the kaleidoscopic patterns of clouds and of the weaving beauty of soughing green branches—all God's good gifts. He had become a Christian and was attending church in his village. My heart was warmed by his joy in the beauty and color and fabric of our furniture and pictures, as he examined them with new and freshly seeing eyes. And he left, after having coffee with me, to go to the work which awaited him—the sharing of God's good gift to him."

JOYOUS ENCOUNTER WITH GOD THROUGH FELLOWSHIP AND WORKING WITH OTHERS

HYMN NO. 276, *The Methodist Hymnal*, "Rise Up, O Men of God"

We all want to belong in our own community. This desire is often more intense in a strange place for the first time. I have always felt that this sense of belonging is one reason why fellowship in the Woman's Society of Christian Service and the Wesleyan Service Guild is of such importance. I discovered this for myself long before I became a staff member of the Woman's Division of Christian Service when I lived in many different places all the way from Florida to California. Wherever I happened to be, I made it a point to attend the meetings of the Woman's Society and the Wesleyan Service Guild, always assured of a warm welcome.

Women in local churches have many opportunities to offer volunteer service in projects of the Board of Missions, often in their own communities. One of my own most memorable experiences of joyous encounter with God has been through working with other Christian women in local churches. Sometimes these were unusual circumstances. While still Director of Christian Education in Christ Church, Methodist, New York City, where Dr. Ralph W. Sockman was the minister, I was asked to serve with the Women's Army Corps at the WAC Training Center in Daytona Beach, Florida.

The assignment was, in some respects, a difficult one. This resort community was the chosen home of many elderly people who had come for rest and quiet in the warm southern climate. Suddenly the Women's Army Corps established a training center there, and the early morning hours were filled with marching girls in uniform and "Hup, two, three, four; hup, two, three, four" resounding in the air. Soda counters usually frequented by visitors from the North were jammed with "lady soldiers."

I was there to serve as civilian liaison officer between the Army Corps and the churches. How could I possibly bring about good relationships between these two groups which seemed so antagonistic? I was only one person. Yet, when I turned to the women of the churches in that community I was amazed at the promptness of their response. I found much misunderstanding on the part of the local residents. Many were convinced that women in uniform had no interest in the church. The reason? Numerous times churches in the community had invited WACs to parties planned especially for them on Friday evenings. Result: no one came. "Obviously they are not interested in the church," the church women insisted. One visit to the post gave me the answer. Saturday morning was "white glove" inspection day when the lieutenant goes over everything with white gloves—even underneath the bed! Uniforms had to be perfectly pressed, shoes polished and lockers in perfect order. Small wonder that none of the girls had time to go anywhere for a Friday night program. As soon as this was understood, churches planned parties at more convenient times and the response was tremendous.

These girls in uniform were not only entertained, but they also provided much enjoyment for the churchgoers. Many WACs taught church school classes, and the WAC choir often sang at religious services. Most significant was the permission given by the commanding officer for the WAC choir to sing at the World Community Day service in our large Methodist church on the Peninsula.

When the Army decided, just two months later, to move the WACs from Daytona to Fort Oglethorpe, Georgia, the very people who had previously objected to the training center were literally in tears that such lovely girls were leaving their community. This happened because the local church women made every effort to meet the needs of these young women away from home. They opened their homes for parties of various kinds, sent things to the girls, even furnished a Santa Claus suit for a WAC Christmas party of the post. In turn, WAC choral groups on Christmas Eve sang carols to shut-ins in the community and sang from boats along the Halifax River.

Again, at Fort Oglethorpe, church women responded to suggestions for making WACs welcome in the community. Here, too, there were invitations to church suppers and into private homes. When Dr. E. Stanley Jones was in nearby Chattanooga on a preaching mission, men of one Methodist church provided bus transportation to the city for the WACs. Women of two other Methodist churches prepared supper in neighboring churches. I recall his surprise as he looked up from the platform and saw the entire balcony filled with WACs. Later, realizing that he was taking up more than the usual time for the evening service, Dr. Jones made a break in his address to give anyone who wanted to leave an opportunity to do so. Not one WAC left the auditorium.

Similar interest and response came from women of the San Francisco Bay area when I was assigned there following World War II to work with new arrivals in the housing projects. I left New York City with considerable trepidation to take this position on the West Coast. Work among people in the desolate temporary homes on the outskirts of Oakland would be difficult. However, as soon as I arrived I found other church women who not only gave me, personally, a warm welcome and many words of encouragement, but who were also eager to assist actively in the program.

Work in these housing projects proved as hard as I had anticipated—in many ways even harder. We were to minister to groups who ranged in age from wee nursery tots to grandmothers. It would have been absolutely impossible to carry out any kind of program alone. As soon as the needs became known, Methodist and other church women cooperated in starting a program against what seemed almost insurmountable difficulties. The local women left their own beautifully equipped churches to help start church activities in these bleak areas. They taught church school classes, helped with vacation church schools, and assisted with music and recreation. They formed motorcades to take women to interesting programs in other parts of the city. At Easter they brought such carloads of lovely lilies that the entire front of the drab room in which our worship services were held became beautiful. The women's group thus started ordinarily met in the tiny combined kitchen-dining-living room of a project home until one imaginative and generous woman opened her attractive home for them!

This spirit of loving fellowship extended far beyond the local community. As the women worked together, their interests and concerns broadened. Offerings taken at the close of our vacation church schools in all five projects were used to send paperback copies of the Bible to Japanese children whose Bibles had been destroyed during World War II. Some years later when I heard the famed Dr. Toyohiko Kagawa, the great Japanese Christian leader speak, he remarked that nothing had so boosted the morale of the Japanese Christians as did the

TO ENCOUNTER

Bibles sent from America. Through such service by local women I saw an ever-widening joyous Christian fellowship of love reaching out to strangers in the community and on to far-distant lands.

JOY IN GIVING AND SHARING

HYMN NO. 466, *The Methodist Hymnal*, "O Brother Man, Fold to Thy Heart Thy Brother"

How often we can learn from children or simple folk some of the most profound lessons of life. There is a special joy that comes to the Christian in sharing with others. We tend to think of missionaries as being particularly adept at this since they are called on to share their faith with those who have not heard of Christ. However, we may all experience this joy when we take our faith seriously enough to be concerned to share it.

What mother has not known the joy of receiving a crumpled flower from grimy little hands? What teacher has not experienced the special joy at the radiant look of sudden understanding and discovery on the face of a child? What adult has not found joy in a simple gift when it was given from the heart?

Not long before her death in India in 1965, Mrs. Marion Riddle, a missionary from New Zealand, shared the following story with friends:

"Our life has had its storm-tossed moments when gifts of rare quality have been thrown to us out of the turbulent sea of days.

"Anne was two and a half when she was burned. I can speak about it now, twelve years later. It happened in our home at the foot of the mountains in North India. There is still the long, incurable sting of memory: the piercing shrieks, the red and yellow flames licking up and curling around her stamping, frenzied little figure, the sixty-five-mile dash to the Ludhiana Hospital. Just the agony and the heartache make raw memories have a nightmare quality. Yet they are tempered with other memories and gifts of kindness, care, and prayers—and in particular, Chetu's gift.

"Chetu is part of the crowd of people who are the poor of India: those uncared-for, dirt-begrimed creatures in grey clothes who are tattered and battered by the toughness of living on nothing. He is unlikely material. But Chetu, too, has had his hour. Chetu had eaten nothing all that day when Anne was burned in the evening. He borrowed money in the bazaar and bought *two dozen eggs* and came running to our door. The cook separated the whites from the yolks and placed them in a clean basin—egg whites is an old Indian cure for burns. Someone placed my hands in the basin of egg whites. What exquisite relief! Only then did I know that my hand was severely burned.

"Chetu had nothing—not even enough for a meal that day. But he gave more than he possessed. He gave *two dozen eggs* which were more precious than gold and silver. I am sure that when Chetu comes before his Maker he will be led by the hand to a place of honor.

"It is God's nature to give. He gives to us as a father gives. He gives, not for our indulgence, but for our fulfillment. It is a fine gift—the gift of the heart that has time and interest and healing and love for another. God is a 'person giver.' He gives Himself and changes lives. This is the greatest gift of all."

EXPRESSING GRATITUDE FOR LIFE'S MANY JOYS

Read Psalm 96 responsively.

How often do we stop to give thanks to God for all of the joys which He has bestowed upon us? I think of the ten lepers who Jesus healed. Only one returned to thank the Master (Luke 17:12-19). Are we like that one, or are we like the nine?

In times of sorrow, God is the one source of strength to whom we can turn. But do we as readily turn to God

TO ENCOUNTER

in our moments of joy? Do we accept just casually the beauty and orderliness of God's universe, the love which surrounds us in our homes, the faithful friends who have so enriched our lives through the years? Do we fail to express our gratitude for the church, the dedicated ministers and church school teachers who introduced us to the study of the Bible and helped to teach us the joy of following in the Christian way?

Elton Watlington, a Methodist missionary, shares his observations on life's small pleasures in a letter which is datelined Lima, Peru, South America. He begins:

"While riding a crowded bus over a gravel road in the high plains of Peru a few weeks ago, I began a list of the small pleasures of life which have become meaningful to me, and which I would like to share with you. It is now a long list—life is filled with so many things: small irritations, satisfactions, and pleasures. The small pleasures of life are sometimes crowded to one side, and yet I am sure these things can be meaningful and give hope when discouragement and sorrow come. This is my list:

> A warm place to sleep
> A drink of cool water on a hot day
> The satisfaction of a full stomach
> Clean clothes
> The caress of a child
> A flower in the desert
> A prayer rising from a sincere heart
> The joy of a neat, clean home
> The laughter of children
> The touch of a friend's hand in time of sorrow and discouragement
> Good news from old friends
> An old pair of shoes and a new friend
> The sight of growing grain for a hungry world
> A hymn of praise from joyful voices

"What is your list? What are the small pleasures of life that are so meaningful to you? In the rustic environment of central Peru, the small pleasures of life are simpler than in many places of the world because the elemental needs of every man are represented here. Again and again we are reminded that we are one people under God and that our needs and our desires are common.

"As there are small pleasures common to all of us, there are also small victories and joys that come in the service of the Lord in Peru. First of all, I would like to tell you of Fermin Casana and of the awakening interest that he has in the church and in the ministry during these past months. About nine months ago I asked Fermin . . . if he would not be interested in sharing in a ministry to one of the squatter districts of Lima at our outpost Sunday school at Comas Kilometer 11. . . .

"What is happening in our Sunday school at Comas Kilometer 11 is a story in itself. The part that has pleased me greatly is what is happening to Fermin in accepting the challenge of the church to give of his free time for this project of witness in greater Lima. What a joy it is to see a fellow Christian accepting responsibility for witnessing to Christ!"

What about your list? Let each one of us silently begin her own list now in these following moments. (Have the pianist play Hymn No. 9, *The Methodist Hymnal*, "My God, I Thank Thee, Who Hast Made the Earth So Bright," as the group sits in meditation on their list. Then conclude by singing the hymn.)

CHRISTIANITY IS A RELIGION OF JOY
Read John 15:11 and 17:13

A Buddhist priest told a professor in a theological seminary that he would never want to become a Christian because all those he had seen so often looked sad, troubled, and worried. Are we guilty of being sorrowful Christians?

It is interesting how many times Jesus uses the word "joy" in his ministry. This joy was meant not only for

TO ENCOUNTER

the disciples of that day but for all who believe in Him. Christians in the early church showed this joy wherever they went. Even in prison, Paul and Silas "were praying and singing hymns, . . ." (Acts 16:25).

The beginning of the Gospel account is an event of joy as the angelic chorus sang the gladsome tidings of Jesus' birth. The closing event is one of joy for the risen Christ when the disciples "returned to Jerusalem with great joy" (Luke 24:52). Those first seventy missionaries whom Jesus sent out "returned with joy" (Luke 10:17).

A Christian is one in whom Christ's joy has been fulfilled (John 17:13). Such a person can't help but spill joy over on others.

A friend of mine was in Southeast Asia for the World Council of Christian Education and attended a worship service in a leper colony. She was deeply moved to hear these poor afflicted people joyously sing the "Hallelujah Chorus." Their joy was indeed full and running over. They had come to know Christ because a missionary had come to share this fullness of joy with them.

Let us make a "joyful noise unto the Lord."

HYMN NO. 12, *The Methodist Hymnal*, "Joyful, Joyful, We Adore Thee"

PRAYER: O God, by whose hand all living things were made, and by whose blessing they are nourished and sustained; we give Thee hearty thanks for all the bounties of Thy providence, wherewith Thou hast enriched our life. Enjoying Thy gifts in contentment, may we be enabled by Thy grace to use them to Thy praise. Especially we thank Thee for Thy great love; in sending Thy Son to be the Savior of the world and in calling us into fellowship with Him; and we beseech Thee to grant us always Thy Holy Spirit; through whom we may grow continually in thankfulness toward Thee; and also into the likeness of Thy Son Jesus Christ, our Lord. Amen.*

* From *The Book of Common Worship* of the Presbyterian Church U.S.A.

TO ENCOUNTER

PIANO POSTLUDE: Soft music while heads are bowed.

RESOURCES

ORDER THE FOLLOWING FROM THE SERVICE CENTER
7820 READING ROAD, CINCINNATI, OHIO 45237

God's Plan for You. Meditation leaflet on the practice of the presence of God in our daily life. 3 cents each; 10 for 25 cents.

To Serve Right Gloriously. Leaflet emphasizing stewardship of mind, time, and energy as well as money. For personal inspiration and meditation or for use in a worship service. Free.

to Invest...

Your "human capital"
for bringing
equal opportunity
for all people
to study
live
work
and worship
with health
and hope
in a free
and just
world

TO INVEST

in the YMCA during the Second World War, I immediately became interested in the students at the Christian Medical College when I went to Ludhiana as the pastor of the United Church of Northern India.

Our church was the unofficial church of the hospital and college staff since we were the closest Protestant church to the hospital compound.

There are three chapel services daily: one is for the nurses, one for the medical students, and the third for patients, relatives, and others who may wish to come. Usually the staff and students take charge of these services although they have a full-time chaplain who is generally responsible for planning. In addition to these services held in the chapel, there are half hour services held on each of the hospital wards every Sunday. These again are conducted by the staff and students.

An interesting outgrowth of this has been the development of a program of literature distribution. Daily, someone goes into the wards with Christian literature to be sold and given away. Many times this avenue of evangelism reaches farther than the formal chapel services because this written word can be carried and passed along many miles from the chapel.

The office of the chaplain is a busy place. Besides having the responsibility for planning chapel services, he also serves as a counselor to students, patients and their relatives, and staff, helping to bridge the gap between fear and hope, anxiety and confidence. We have students from many backgrounds, and they often find the first months difficult. Adjusting to institutional life is never easy.

We are thrilled with the increasing numbers of Christian students who qualify for entrance into the medical college, nurses' training, and technician training programs offered at Ludhiana. I believe that forty-four per cent of the new class admitted in 1964 were Christians. This is an increase of almost ten per cent over the previ-

TO INVEST

fall sadly on the three preschoolers playing in the doorway. They wait for the father who will never come.

Oaxaca, Mexico: A lonely child sits for hours on a steep mountainside holding a piece of stone to sell as a "relic" of ancient ruins.

Dublin, Ireland: A ten-year-old with dirty blond curls and a smudged face walks the streets at 10 P.M., a bundle of papers under her arm—in a hoarse voice cries the headlines.

Each wears the face of pain, hunger, hopelessness, fear—the hollow look, the mask of poverty.

SPEAKER III: How does poverty feel? Is it the same in Latin America, Asia, Africa, the U.S.A.? If we could hear a voice speaking from behind the mask, what would it say?

It is afternoon in a rural village in India . . .

SCENE I: (*An Indian woman with an earthen cup similar to a bowl enters. She is wearing a sari and is barefoot. She sits down on the floor.*)

INDIAN MOTHER: Kamala, poor daughter, cursed to be born a girl. Thirteen years and no dowry, except these few brass cooking pans. Her father loves her, but he complains about the day he will have to provide her wedding feast. He need not worry; she probably will never marry. Who will marry a girl who has only a few brass cooking pans even when she's pretty?

The drought destroyed our rice crop. If it doesn't rain, the rice doesn't grow. We have to guard every mouthful of food until the next harvest. How can five of us survive on so little food?

My small son Raj is so frail. If he doesn't get enough to eat now, he may not live. He is so smart and loves school. Soon Jaswant will finish school. If he would only stay here and work in the village or marry, then Kamala could have a dowry. He's stronger than the rest; maybe he'll survive, but he won't be much help to us. He wants to go to the city—be a clerk, he says.

TO INVEST

I am afraid of the city. I think my husband would like to go with Jaswant, but I am afraid. I know this village; I know the land. Sometimes the harvest is good. Maybe it will be next year. (*The woman rises and leaves the stage.*)

SPEAKER III: (*A woman in a plain cotton dress, shabby and unkempt, walks onto the stage and sits down at the table. She is barefoot. She picks up the cup, takes a drink, and leans back.*)

BRAZILIAN MOTHER: My son will be angry when he gets home tonight. Nothing but black beans and rice. How he loves meat, that growing boy. He seldom tastes it; I don't know how he could like it so well.

Lucky I found that pair of shoes in the trash can. Carlos can wear the left one and José the right. It's a little big for him, but it will do. A bandage on each bare foot, and the school will be satisfied. I don't know why they insist on shoes. Me, I am used to bare feet.

My boys are good boys even with no father to make them listen. There is always crime and trouble in this neighborhood, but I see that they don't use the foul language of the *favelas*. We may live in a shack and have little soap, but we don't have filthy mouths!

I try to keep busy, but I can't avoid hearing all the gossip when I lug my pail to the spigot for water. The line is so long and those women chatter so!

My day begins and ends with my search for trash to sell—papers and metal. Someday I will know what it means to see my children smile and say, "We've had enough to eat, Mama." (*The woman rises and leaves the stage.*)

SPEAKER III: The scene turns to a coal mining town in West Virginia—Appalachia. (*Woman with modest cotton dress walks in. She sits down at the table; occasionally she takes a sip of coffee.*)

APPALACHIAN MOTHER: Bill should be home from the post office soon. I hope the welfare check came today.

183

TO INVEST

I bought any food. For three hours I stood in lines at the market. If I want good food at cheap prices, I have to keep looking. I'm so tired now that I don't see how I can get this piecework finished for the factory tomorrow. A little of this parched corn tea may be just what I need. (*She sips tea from a porcelain cup.*)

So many new refugees keep moving into our area. Most of the homes around here are made of tin, gasoline cans and boxes. It doesn't take long to put up another shack—and another and another. Almost every family lives in just one room like this. One room for six of us is crowded even though the kitchen is a lean-to outside.

With millions of refugees, work is hard to find. My husband has no education, and he cleans streets. My sons are going to school. When they graduate, they may have to clean streets if there aren't more jobs by then. But they must go to school whatever the future brings. They cannot become beggars.

There is so much fighting here in shack land. Even women pull each other's hair when they are angry. I cannot be this way.

I spent so much time at the market this morning I didn't get water for tonight. That means a long wait at the water spigot. It can't be any colder outside than it is in.

Dirt floors, no furniture, and no heat. I wonder why life is so hard. My husband never asks such a question. But mothers have to when they have children to think about. (*She rises and leaves the stage.*)

SPEAKER III: And back in the United States in the heart of Chicago's West Side slums . . .

SCENE VI: (*A woman with a waitress uniform enters. She sits down at the table and begins to sip on a cup of coffee.*)

CHICAGO MOTHER: Jimmy sure looked happy to get that money. One hot dog and a cup of pop; that is a fine meal as far as he is concerned. Besides, then he has a chance to talk to the hot dog man. He likes talking to him. Makes up some for not having a father around. His father would never have noticed him anyway. He left us when Jimmy was just learning to crawl. I don't know where he went, and now I don't care.

I don't make much as a waitress, but it keeps Jimmy and me going. So sometimes we haven't got much! Jimmy never complains about hot dogs. I'm too beat to get him a good hot meal most of the time. Even if I wasn't, we couldn't afford much.

I wish I had a home, a nice place for Jimmy, instead of this apartment with the walls cracking and dirt everywhere. But it doesn't look like I can ever afford much more than we've got right now.

Everyone around here is sick inside craving something he can't have. Sure, welfare checks come in handy for many, but they pay for necessities, not dreams.

Some people get out of here and make good. Some just drink or take dope. Then they don't notice what it is really like. My life and ambition are pinned on Jimmy. I hope he doesn't stay on the streets too long tonight. Maybe he will eat and come right home. Now that he is growing up, I am afraid for him. There is too much crime on this street, and no place for nice kids to go. Gee, I wish Jimmy would hurry home. Maybe tomorrow I'll make him a meal at home.

SPEAKER III: How many times have you said casually, "I wish I weren't so poor"? How do you compare your needs with the needs of these mothers? Why is the United States often referred to as the "affluent society"? What do we consider to be necessities that would be a luxury for the women we've just met? Has our only contact with poverty been when we put together food baskets for distribution at Thanksgiving and Christmas?

"My brothers, what use is it for a man to say he has faith when he does nothing to show it? Can that faith save him? Suppose a brother or a sister is in rags with

Opportunity to Study

VIRGINIA LAW

PURPOSE: To discover how the investment by the church of "human capital" is helping bring equal opportunities to study.

PRE-PROGRAM PLANNING:

You may wish to simplify the suggested "scene settings." One alternative would be to locate the home of each of these three students on a world map and prepare picture posters to illustrate life in the three countries.

Accessories which would be interesting to use with the program are listed on page 205.

PROGRAM PRESENTATION:

PRAYER:

Spirit of life and love, Come to us and fill us.
Spirit of truth and power, Change us and use us.
Spirit of growth and grace, Come like a wind and cleanse us.
Come as a fire to burn, Stab us awake to reality.
(Clarice Bowman, *Resources for Worship*, New York: Association Press, New York, page 128.)

HYMN: No. 477, *The Methodist Hymnal*, "Let There Be Light."

SCRIPTURE: John 15:1-17.

LEADER: In our secular life we are familiar with the word *mission*. Its definition, "a sending forth," gives us no problem of understanding as we hear of peace missions,

TO INVEST

rescue missions, relief missions, or space missions. The difference between any of these missions is in their aims. As a church we face yet another mission. *The Methodist Discipline* states clearly: "The supreme aim of missions is to make the Lord Jesus Christ known to all peoples in all lands as their Divine Savior." We are engaged in this task around the world. As a church we go forth to bring about an encounter between persons and Christ that will make a difference in their lives.

Today we would like you to meet some of the people who have been influenced by the missionary outreach of our church. While some of us must "role play" for this program, let us remember that the words are based on actual interviews with students at Scarritt College, Nashville, Tennessee.

(NOTE TO LEADER: *You will find here a suggestion of possible stage settings. Costuming will have to be adapted to what is available. Though it is not necessary, it will enrich the program. At the front have three scenes set up: Fiji Islands, India, and Japan.*)

Scene I: Fiji Islands

Stage setting: Light blue background with fish netting draped across. Shells in this netting. Large green plants sitting about to create a tropical atmosphere. Large vases of yellow and red flowers. A cane table and two chairs.
LORINE *wears a bright floral dress with a full skirt. Under this, drape around the hips a long, solid-colored cloth which hangs to the ankles. Around the head a bright headband. Shell earrings or pins are appropriate.*
LEADER (*going to the appropriate stage area*): Our first guest today is Miss Lorine Chan from the Fiji Islands. The British Wesleyan Methodists were the first Western missionaries in these islands, in 1835. However, we Methodists in the United States do participate in the development of the church there. Miss Chan, a member of The Methodist Church of Australasia, attends Scarritt

TO INVEST

College on a Crusade Scholarship provided by American Methodists. Miss Chan, will you please tell us something about the Fiji Islands and where they are?

LORINE: I would be glad to tell you about my home. The islands are in the South Pacific, about 17-20° south of the equator, east of Australia and north of New Zealand. Our population is quite international, with Indians and Fijians in the majority, then Europeans and others from the Southeast Asian and Pacific lands. The whole land area is more than seven thousand square miles—a little bigger than the combined size of Connecticut and Rhode Island. The population is less than five hundred thousand.

LEADER: You say that the islands are multiracial?

LORINE: Yes. I myself represent two races: my father was Chinese and my mother was a native Fijian. My father came from China as a child. He met my mother through some of his friends, and they were married in a civil marriage service. They were later divorced, which is unusual in our culture.

LEADER: Could you share with us what happened?

LORINE: My mother married my father to escape from the "arranged marriage" which my grandfather had worked out for her. She was never happy with my father. When she remarried, my sister and I went to live with her.

LEADER: Did you live in a city, a town, or a village?

LORINE: We lived in the city although our grandparents lived in the village.

LEADER: What is a village like in Fiji?

LORINE: Well, the farmers live grouped together in a community. Each farmer has his own plot, but he doesn't buy it—the land belongs to the community, which is really an extended family or clan. All the farmer has to do is clear and cultivate it. Then it is his. Only a few European farmers or land owners live as farmers do in the United States.

LEADER: Isn't it true that your people had no written language until the missionaries came, and that the early missionaries started village schools wherever they went? What kind of education did you have?

LORINE: Because of the British Methodist missionaries there is a very high percentage of literacy among Fijians. Those first schools were mostly in villages, but they grew into high schools. When the government assumed responsibility for the educational system in 1930, the church-sponsored schools began to emphasize special types of training.

LEADER: Did you take all your schooling in one school?

LORINE: I took my first five grades in a small, local school. Then I attended the Davuilevu (dah-vi-lay-voo) Educational Center, which the Methodists started in 1856. The center offers primary, secondary, technical, and theological education in its various schools. I went to high school there and attended a state teacher-training college.

LEADER: Was that a four-year college?

LORINE: No, actually it is only two years of specialized training for teachers of grades one to eight. It isn't like the liberal arts course that I'm now taking at Scarritt and Peabody.

LEADER: Do you notice many differences between your school and our American schools?

LORINE: Yes. The first difference I noticed was that students don't work in the school here in America. In Fiji our fees are very low, but every student has to work in the school. We do our own cooking, cleaning, and washing; and the boys raise much of the food on a school plantation. There are no servants in our schools. This is in the boarding schools, some of which are from grade five to senior high and others from grade seven to senior high. Even in the day and district schools, children do light work like cleaning the school grounds and such jobs.

LEADER: You say you attended a Methodist school. I'd be interested in knowing why you chose this school.

LORINE: This is one of the few mission schools on the island. My parents were Christians, and they would have wanted me to attend a Christian school.

LEADER: Knowing that missionaries have been in the Fiji Islands more than one hundred years, I wonder if you know how many generations of your family have been Christians?

LORINE: I'm the third generation.

LEADER: Are you a Christian because you grew up in a Christian home?

LORINE: Partially so. Certainly I could never get away from the influence of my parents and grandparents who were devoted Christians and helped lead me, but I had to make my own decision about whether to be a Christian or not. I guess there are really no second-generation Christians there. Each one of us must decide for himself.

LEADER: Could you tell us how you made your decision?

LORINE: Yes, I'd like to share it with you. At my school in Davuilevu there is a large church called the Baker Church. From my earliest childhood I had heard the story of the Reverend Thomas Baker. He came to Fiji in the second half of the nineteenth century as a missionary. Shortly after arriving he went with several Fijian catechists to a mountain village, leaving his wife and family at the school. Unfortunately he went to an area where the Fijians were still cannibals, and they killed and ate him. In spite of this, the British Methodist Christians continued to send money and support to my country and built Baker Church in honor of him.

Sitting there one Sunday morning, hearing again the story of Thomas Baker, I looked up at the tall vaulted ceiling of the church and thought, "What a wonderful place to worship." Then behind the pulpit I noticed the large brass cross shining and below it the names of other early missionaries. I began to read and my eyes rested on the name Thomas Baker. It seemed that morning that his name stood out; and I began to think of Fiji as I knew it, and Fiji as he had found it. I could hardly believe the difference. I knew the love of God had sent

Jesus to us. But this love had come to Fiji through Baker and other dedicated Christians. If he could bring so much from a strange land, what could I, a native Fijian, do? I opened my heart and accepted Christ and gave my life to Him to bring this love to others of my own land.

LEADER: What a beautiful story to have come out of such a tragic death.

LORINE: Yes, Thomas Baker's death was tragic; but I feel that if he could see how Fiji has changed because of Christ, he would not have regretted dying in such a way.

LEADER: Thank you for sharing this with us. Few have to make such a sacrifice as Thomas Baker. How we need to examine our own Christian commitment to consider how much we are willing to sacrifice!

Scene II: India

Stage setting: Hang a rug, drape, or bedspread with deep vivid colors for a background. The LEADER *and* LEELA *will sit on the floor with legs crossed. Put a rug on the floor for them, and place a brass or copper vase on the rug with brightly colored leaves arranged about it. Wrap gold foil around a goblet to simulate brass drinking goblets.*

The sari is the traditional dress of Indian women. For this wear a slip and short blouse with a belt at the waist. Take a six-yard length of 42-inch cloth of any kind or color provided it will drape easily. Place one end of cloth at right of center front and pin in place. Wrap the cloth completely around, going from left to right and back to left of center. Holding the cloth away from the body make six deep 4-inch pleats, one on top of the other. Pin these together and tuck top edge over the belt. Continue the cloth on around the left hip and back, lifting it higher under the right arm; drape it across the bust and around the back, throwing the remaining cloth over the left shoulder. Pin with a bright pin at shoulder. Wear bracelets, beads, and earrings. If possible, have a wig of long black hair tied back in a knot to be truly Indian.

LEADER: From Fiji we now come to India where we will visit with Miss Leela Jacobs. The first thing that catches my eye is the lovely sari which she is wearing. Would you explain to us how this is made and worn, Leela? (LEELA *demonstrates her sari if she is wearing one. If not, omit the comments which refer to it.*)

LEELA: This is only one of many ways of wearing a sari. In different parts of India they drape it in various ways. It is our national dress, although a few very modern working girls in cities may sometimes wear Western dress.

LEADER: They certainly are very beautiful and graceful. I have always admired Indian women wearing them. Where is your home in India?

LEELA: I come from Bidar (beed-ur) in south India. My village is in a valley surrounded by hills, and the path down into the village is very rocky and steep.

LEADER: Have you lived there all your life?

LEELA: No, I haven't. My father was a Methodist preacher so we moved from village to village, never having a home of our own. But I claim Bidar as home because that was where my paternal grandfather lived.

LEADER: You say your father was a preacher. Do you know what influenced him to enter the ministry?

LEELA: It's a familiar story in our family. The greatest influence was his own father. Years ago my grandfather was a very devout Hindu priest who conducted the Hindu rites in his own home. When he saw Hindu men were having problems in coming to worship in his home, he looked for another place to meet. On a hill some distance from the village he found a rocky ledge, but it was too narrow for all the people to meet on. With his own hands my grandfather began to carve out a chapel into the side of the hill. Every evening the Hindu worshipers gathered here for their vesper service.

TO INVEST

LEADER: Was it this devotion of your grandfather's to Hinduism that influenced your father?

LEELA: In his early life, yes. My father could see how much this worship meant to his father. One day all this changed. A missionary visited Bidar with his silent pictures of Christ's life and a Gramophone with records. Along with all the other villagers my grandfather went to see them. An Indian interpreter traveled with the missionary, explaining the pictures. My grandfather stayed to ask questions after the service, and that night he went home and pondered the message. He knew he would have many difficulties if he became a Christian. Still he could not resist the claim he felt Christ made upon his heart. The next morning he and his wife became Christians, the first in our village.

LEADER: Did he have difficulties after becoming a Christian?

LEELA: Yes, he really did suffer. The village people rebuked him. The other Hindu priests and worshipers disowned him. When my grandfather was instrumental in bringing three of his brothers and their wives to accept Christ, the entire village became aroused. They forbade my grandparents to draw water at the village well. No one would work in their fields as hired hands. No one invited them to any feast or celebrations at weddings or other happy occasions in the village.

LEADER: Did these actions affect your grandfather?

LEELA: Yes, they did. He suffered greatly. Village life in India is very important. His neighbors' rejection was painful to him, but he didn't give up his new-found faith. Instead of weakening, he began to follow the missionary about, trying to learn more. He worked hard to make the old Hindu chapel even bigger to use for Christian worship.

LEADER: Did he become a preacher?

LEELA: No, he remained a layman; but I remember he was always going somewhere to help someone. My grandmother was left with most of the field work to oversee because grandfather was always away on some errand of mercy.

LEADER: Did the persecution in his village continue?

LEELA: For a long time it did, but gradually the people began to see that there really was something different in my grandfather's life; and one by one they became Christians. They filled the little stone chapel for their worship. Grandfather also went to other villages, and Christian converts in all areas knew him. Now, on Good Friday and Easter Sunday of each year, crowds come from long distances, sometimes as many as three thousand people, to worship in and around the chapel on the hill.

LEADER: Did your grandfather live to see this?

LEELA: No, he didn't. He died in a bubonic plague epidemic which killed many people. I think it is a challenge for me, his granddaughter, to remember that at the time he died, this plague did not reach our village. He became ill while serving the sick people in another village some distance from our home.

LEADER: It is easy to understand how your father was inspired to become a preacher with such an influence in his life. I suppose it was only natural for you to grow up in the church because of this heritage.

LEELA: I don't remember when I first went to church, but I went to our Methodist mission schools from the first grade through high school, and then finished my college at Isabella Thoburn College. All of these made an impression on me, but looking back I can see the influence of my grandfather and my father even more strongly upon my life.

I grew up with a desire to be a Christian. When I was in the fourth grade, I asked the missionary if I could please have a Bible for Christmas instead of a toy. She gave me a beautiful one with black and gold binding. I remember what I had written in my very unsteady handwriting on the flyleaf of this Bible: "Lord, teach me to pray." I wrapped the book in cloth and guarded it very carefully, but several years later it was lost. I still feel sad when I think of losing my Bible.

LEADER: Did you have any unusual experience when you became a Christian?

LEELA: I can't remember an exact time when I became a Christian, but I do remember when I first realized how real and powerful a faith in Christ was. I had a terrible illness when I was away at school. For several days the nurses were very concerned about me. Lying there, feeling alone, I lifted my heart in prayer and faith. The next time the nurse checked my fever, it had started to lower. This was important to them, and no doubt the drugs and care they had given me helped; but more important to me was the deep sense of peace and security which I felt after praying. There are three times in my life when I have been wonderfully healed from a serious illness.

LEADER: This vital faith of which you speak certainly has been evident in your life. After college you taught in the high school where you had graduated. Later you came to America and received your M.A. at Syracuse University. Where were you teaching before you came here to Scarritt?

LEELA: I've been on the staff at Leonard Theological College in Jubalpur. You American Methodists are helping provide scholarships for some students from the Fiji Islands who are attending this Methodist school. The "connectional" lines of our church working through The Methodist Church in Southern Asia, in India, of Australasia, and in the United States are helping develop leadership for the church in both India and in Fiji.

LEADER: Teaching in a school like that must be both rewarding and challenging.

LEELA: Yes, it is; but I have had a good example to follow. I saw in the life of my grandfather a deep dedication to service. As I grew up, I learned from the life of Jesus this same sense of service. Then as I began to work, I

TO INVEST

realized for myself that there is real peace in feeling you are serving where you are needed.
LEADER: Some of us might envy you this sense of peace.

Scene III: Japan

Stage setting: Form a background using a bamboo screen or some neutral beige material. Any prints from Japan could be hung on this, or silhouette figures of flowers cut from black construction paper could decorate it. Place a low table in the center with a bright colored cushion on each side. On the table place a low round teapot and cups. AKIKO *can be dressed in any straight floral shift with a mandarin collar.*

LEADER: When I think of Japan, I think of beautiful Mount Fuji as I have seen it in pictures, or of lovely flower arrangements. I'm sure you would agree that Japan is a beautiful country.
AKIKO: Yes, we Japanese think so, and most visitors agree.
LEADER: We are now interviewing Miss Akiko Yajima, from Yokohama in the eastern part of Japan. The first interesting thing about you, Akiko, is that I understand you were born in a Buddhist temple. Sometimes here in America we hear of babies being born in taxicabs or theaters, so I wonder how you came to be born in a Buddhist temple?
AKIKO: Well, since my father's father was a Buddhist priest, my family lived in the temple; and I was born there.
LEADER: Actually, then, you were born at the home of your parents which happened to be in the Buddhist temple where your grandfather was a priest.
AKIKO: Yes. This was the home of my parents, but not just the home of our family as you think of it in America. Here two or three generations of our family all lived together with my grandfather and grandmother. Grandfather was a priest and grandmother was the head or

TO INVEST

controlling factor in the family.

LEADER: Then I'm sure you were raised in the Buddhist faith.

AKIKO: From my earliest childhood I began to learn the Buddhist scriptures. It is a very strict discipline.

LEADER: How long did you live in the temple?

AKIKO: Until my father moved to Yokohama to become a research botanist at the college. I was then about twelve years old, and this was a big change for us. Father's family objected because they wanted him to become the Buddhist priest; but Father insisted upon being a botanist, and the family was very upset.

LEADER: Why was this so?

AKIKO: Because he was the oldest son and, according to our tradition, would be responsible for my grandmother's well-being. The offerings at the temple would bring more money to support the family than Father would receive as a botanist. When we moved from the temple, we had to look for another school for me to attend. I had been educated in the temple until this time. My father chose to send me to a Methodist mission school—an even bigger change than moving from the temple!

LEADER: I'm sure this would be so. But why did your father send you to a mission school?

AKIKO: It was an old school which had been established by an American missionary eighty-eight years before. The academic standards were very high and there were excellent missionary teachers. Also, the school had maintained a high moral level in the society. Being a college professor, my father recognized this. Everyone knew that the students at this school were different from those in public school.

LEADER: What was your first impression when you reached the school after coming from the Buddhist temple?

AKIKO: My first experience was in the chapel service. I looked around in amazement as the older students stood singing the hymns. The atmosphere was worshipful, and they seemed so happy. Their worship seemed to come from their hearts. I could remember sitting on that wooden floor in the temple. Here we were peaceful and serene with such a freedom to worship.

My second impression was of the missionaries. They were Americans, but they had a wonderful influence at that time just after World War II. They devoted themselves to religious education, and we were very thankful for them. I began to get close to these missionaries, watching them, listening to them when they talked, and always asking myself one question: "What is the secret of this life of service?"

LEADER: I gather that this was an influence which grew as you attended school.

AKIKO: Yes, it did; and one day I decided that I wanted this same spirit in my life. I shall always remember what a missionary said in that worship service: "The most important decision that you as students must make is the decision as to what you want to do with your life. If you are not a Christian, you must decide if you really want to be. If you are a Christian, you must choose as your lifework whatever you can be of the greatest service in, in the kingdom of God. If your talent is for business, you must go into business and serve God there. If you choose teaching, you must remember that the most important thing is to teach the gospel of Jesus. No matter what you do, you must not think of yourself first but of the service you can give the world for God. You must forget yourself and think of the need. Seek to find the place in which your service is most needed."

Listening to her I decided two things: First, I really wanted to be a Christian; and second, I wanted to find my place of service. I asked my father for permission to become a Christian.

LEADER: Was this a surprise to him?

AKIKO: Yes, he didn't think that after all my Buddhist

training I would change. He had wanted me merely to study at the mission and had not expected me to become a Christian.

LEADER: What did he say?

AKIKO: He refused permission. My grandmother insisted that our family was Buddhist, and I could not get permission from her either.

LEADER: What did you do then?

AKIKO: I decided that my first place of service was with my parents to show my behavior as a Christian until I got permission for baptism. Since my teacher knew the Japanese tradition of obedience to parents, he agreed with me that if I really wanted to become a Christian, I didn't have to be baptized—I could simply surrender my heart and accept Christ by faith. If I really wanted to serve God, then my family was the best place to begin. I should go home and be the best Christian I could be so they would know what a Christian really was. Sometimes I wanted to be baptized in secret, but my conscience always prevented this. The missionary began to pray with me that my parents would change their minds.

LEADER: And did they?

AKIKO: Yes, but not for two long years. It was the hardest place I could have served because my grandmother did not want me to become a Christian. I was the first convert from Buddhism to Christianity in my family. I don't really know why they changed their minds. Sometimes they made it hard for me to go to the worship services, but they didn't try to stop me. For two years I lived the life of a secret Christian. I told my father that I didn't want to be a Christian against his will, but I didn't want to be Jesus' child in secret either. Being a Christian in secret really bothered me. I felt I couldn't really serve God and have a vital Christian witness until I came out of hiding. Finally my father gave permission, and I think the happiest day of my

TO INVEST

whole life was when I stood at Christmas time and was baptized.

LEADER: Listening to you makes me appreciate my own baptism. (*Going to a comfortable, very American chair, the* LEADER *continues.*)

LEADER: After talking with these Christians from other countries we are left with many more questions we would like to ask. But our interview is not complete. There is yet one more thing we need. Let us now interview you. Think of yourself now as sitting while Lorine, Leela, and Akiko ask you a few questions. What are your answers?

(*Each of those who took the parts of Lorine, Leela, and Akiko ask the following questions in turn.*)

• Christian missionaries have introduced education in many parts of the world. What do you feel distinguishes education in a Christian school from that received in a government, secular school?

• What has been the relationship of the mission program of the church with the development of higher education in India? Japan? Other countries?

• If you lived in the Fiji Islands, India, or Japan would you choose to attend a Christian school? Why? (Or would you select such a school for your children to attend?)

• We represent people who have come to Christ out of animism, Hinduism, and Buddhism. How do you think a person in a secular society like yours experiences a different (or similar) one to ours?

• In what ways are the challenges to be Christian the same (or different) in my home community and yours?

• How does your Christian faith make a difference in your life? Would your neighbors accept Christ by what they see in your daily life?

RESOURCES
ORDER THE FOLLOWING FROM THE SERVICE CENTER
7820 READING ROAD, CINCINNATI, OHIO 45237

TO INVEST

This Makes the Difference. A presentation of the results of the Crusade Scholarship Program. 17 minutes, color, 33⅓ rpm record. Sale only $4.00.

Japan. Pictorial leaflet on work in Japan. Free.

Japan—A New Profile. Color, pictures, map. 8 pages. Free.

ORDER THE FOLLOWING FROM THE WRIGHT STUDIO
5264 BROOKVILLE ROAD, INDIANAPOLIS, INDIANA 46219

Nationalities Favors. See "The World Our Parish."

Global Napkin. Globe surrounded by sketches of heads of people of twenty-seven nationalities. 50 for 80 cents.

World Flags Centerpiece. See "The World Our Parish." $1.50 each.

Facts Sheet. Provides facts about fifty new nations for conversation topics with foreign students and others. 10 cents.

New Nations Creative Uses. Many ideas for special programs and fellowship with foreign students. 15 cents.

ABOUT THE AUTHOR

See biographical sketch at the end of "United with Women Everywhere."

FOCUS ON WORLD HEALTH:

The Church and the United Nations

MARGARET R. BENDER

PURPOSES: To gain a better understanding of the work of the United Nations.

To discover how the church invests in and cooperates with various UN agencies toward bringing equal opportunity for all people to live, work, and study in health and hope in a free and just world.

PRE-PROGRAM PLANNING:

You will want to obtain or make ahead of time some posters and other materials about the work of the United Nations. Most magazines frequently have articles that could be used for resource.

A world map or a globe may be helpful. It could also serve as the center of your worship setting. Perhaps you will want to locate the WHO centers around the world on the map.

Your worship period might more appropriately come at the close of the program.

PROGRAM PRESENTATION:

(*A group of four women are in the midst of a discussion as we join them.*)

FIRST WOMAN: And so I said to the missionary who was showing us the hospital, "What do you think of having a UNICEF-WHO malaria and yaws station just half a mile down the road?"

SECOND WOMAN: How did you dare? I'd never have had the courage. Did she bite your head off?

THIRD WOMAN: What a thing to say. I'm sure missionaries aren't like that; besides, why should she get upset when you asked her about a health station that was close to her hospital?

SECOND WOMAN: Why wouldn't she resent it? Missions have been doing the job of curing people and building hospitals and training nurses and doctors in that country for a hundred years, and now here comes the UN and wants to get in on the act. Why wouldn't she resent it?

FIRST WOMAN: Hush, you two. Stop arguing about something you don't understand, and let me tell you what actually happened. The missionary said, "It's a new day for us. Through them we are now able to get all the penicillin and sulfa we need, and sometimes other supplies as well. We are thankful for such valuable supplies and gladly keep records for them on the number of yaws and malaria cases that come to our clinic. It's a small service to give them for all their help."

SECOND WOMAN: I can't imagine a missionary doctor feeling like that. After all, the UN and all these new agencies can't give what our missionary doctors and nurses give.

THIRD WOMAN: I wonder whether they think they can. I think perhaps they understand better than you think they do.

FIRST WOMAN: If anyone is interested, I'd be glad to finish my story. I followed up my interview with Doctor White by going down to the UNICEF-WHO station and asking them how they felt about being so close to the mission hospital. They couldn't say enough about how much the mission station meant to them personally, and how much they valued the cooperative relationship.

SECOND WOMAN: I guess I was a little hasty. I jumped at the conclusion that you were talking about some sort of a United Nations thing—isn't UNICEF the one that has the greeting cards?

FOURTH WOMAN: You weren't making a mistake at that point. UNICEF was the abbreviation for the United Nations International Children's Emergency Fund—now it's just called the UN Children's Fund. WHO is the World

Health Organization. They often work together, or, to be more accurate, UNICEF often assists programs that are carried out by the World Health Organization. If you'll forgive me, I think your mistake was in not understanding how organizations, for the most part, see the joy of dealing with the world's health program as one that has room for everyone who wants to help. Also, I think our missionaries can use all the help they can get—even from programs which haven't been there as long as they have.

FIRST WOMAN: That's what I decided, too. In fact, we have a bishop in our church who pointed out that technical assistance like that given by World Health is a new dimension of missions. Just because our missionaries reached that part of Africa nearly a hundred years ago doesn't mean we've finished the job. Through this trip I discovered how often missionaries are asked for advice. They appreciate work that can be started because of agencies like WHO.

THIRD WOMAN: I heard a story about cooperation between mission and World Health programs the other day. Someone asked an official of a regional program whether or not he felt World Health could make major progress in eradicating leprosy from his region during the next ten years. Do you know what he said? He said, "Yes, with the help of the missionaries."

SECOND WOMAN: I knew there would be a catch in it somewhere. So the churches are supposed to put up the money and, no doubt, build the hospitals, too.

THIRD WOMAN: That wasn't what he meant at all! He said the problem with leprosy control was really one of gaining the confidence of the people who had unreported lepers—often children—in their families. In the past, many families were completely separated when some members were put into leper colonies to protect the others from contagion. Often these old experiences were ones that persisted in people's memories and made them afraid to report new cases. Now, however, there are mobile treatment stations which can conduct a program of arresting leprosy and making it noncontagious without removing these new cases from their families.

The help this World Health doctor was looking for from the missionaries was the understanding they could give to the people who had known and trusted them for a long time. He believed the missionaries could help people believe what the doctors were saying. It has worked out that way in many places, too.

FOURTH WOMAN: Let's stop our conversation there, pertinent as it is, and begin the study of the World Health Organization we had planned for today. (*She turns to include the rest of the group.*) I think most of us are ready by now. I'll tell you something about it, and then you can ask some questions.

Suppose we go back to the beginning. The World Health Organization is the United Nations' specialized agency working specifically in the field of health. What a big job that is on a worldwide basis! Until I began to work on this program, I had never thought how much disease has been a factor in the world's history. I discovered that because of disease, great empires have crumbled, armies have faltered in what looked like certain victory, and some races of mankind have totally disappeared!

I also found that, in spite of all the advances medical science has made in the last century, disease still takes an annual toll of lives much greater than the sum of all those killed in wars and accidents. This is very strange, really, because today disease is largely preventable. The sad fact is that in many places there are not the proper facilities for controlling it. Our churches started medical missions in an effort to bring such facilities to people who needed them so desperately. These have been tremendous pioneering projects; but, as much as they wanted to, they were not winning the battle against disease.

Such concern was triggered by the realization that disease is no respecter of persons or of geographical and political frontiers. If this is fully understood, it is easier to recognize that the spread of disease anywhere in the world is everybody's concern and everybody's danger. In the last few decades, rapid transportation has made this even more striking than it was before. Any one of us may rub elbows with someone in a department store or a crowded street who was halfway around the world three days ago. It's easy to see that if there are epidemics in some of the places from which these travelers might have come, those epidemics are a real danger to us.

This is why we should all be concerned about two phases of the worldwide health problem. The first of these is fighting disease wherever it occurs. This isn't an easy task, but we can already chalk up many victories.

The experience of our missionary doctor in Africa isn't unique. Some diseases that used to cause a great deal of human suffering have actually been wiped out in large areas of the world. On their way to the UNICEF Board Meeting held in Bangkok, Thailand, in January, 1964, several groups stopped to see UNICEF-aided projects. They reported that health officials were having difficulty finding cases of yaws and malaria, which had formerly been a health problem. The systematic eradication of these diseases is simply making it a rarity.

(*From the group the* FIFTH WOMAN *raises her hand and asks a question.*)

FIFTH WOMAN: Someone told me a ridiculous story about how it is possible to cure yaws with a few cents worth of penicillin. Do you know anything about that?

FOURTH WOMAN: It is perfectly true. In spite of the dreadful picture of sores and even crippling that an advanced case of yaws presents, it is possible to cure most cases with one shot of penicillin. Bought wholesale on the world market as WHO and UNICEF do, the penicillin costs only a few cents. Even the stubborn cases that require two or three injections don't run up much of a bill.

Eradicating malaria costs a little more because you not only need to treat individual cases but also to drain swamps and destroy the insects that carry the infection. To do this is troublesome and expensive, but I haven't heard of any country that did not consider it worthwhile to carry their share of the expense when help was offered to them through the World Health Organization.

THIRD WOMAN: Since we've started asking questions, I'd like to get one in here. I always hear about give-away programs. In fact, many people in my neighborhood are against any foreign aid, even mission projects, because they think people should help themselves. I always remind them not to lump missionary programs with foreign aid when they make criticisms like that because we bring something else—Christianity. But I think that all the rest is give-away. Now you tell us about countries being glad to do their share when they are helped by these health programs. What do you mean?

FOURTH WOMAN: I'm so glad that you brought that up. I believe you will find an increasing desire on the part of the church people in what we have called "missionary lands" to assume, as rapidly as possible, financial as well as other responsibilities for programs both in the fields of evangelism and of social welfare.

In this way, too, they are like the people who get assistance from United Nations agencies. The UN has some guide lines which help governments in recipient countries feel responsible. UNICEF, for example, requires that the receiving country match the UNICEF aid.

SECOND WOMAN: How can they do that? I thought they were short of money.

FOURTH WOMAN: Most of them are, particularly of what we call "hard currency"—money that is easily accepted on the world market. What these countries often do is furnish items that are known as the "local costs" of a program. This means the salaries of people who work on the programs, housing for United Nations personnel, office space, and other things which are easier to furnish than money, but which mean just as much in the total picture.

Just as missionaries often say that their job is to work themselves out of a job, UN agencies often give preference to necessary projects which can be taken over by governments or voluntary agencies within a reasonable length of time.

For example, I don't think there are any brass plates in the world that are more exciting than two I've seen in Bangkok. One of them is in the tuberculosis hospital. It says that the building was built, the hospital equipped, and the original staff trained or up-graded through UN assistance; and that the hospital is now maintained by the government of Thailand.

The other is in the Pasteur Institute, where snakes are milked for their venom and antitoxins are prepared. Here, too, UN agencies made the institute possible and helped maintain it until the government and certain local funds were able to take it over. UNICEF helped a great deal in this project because death from snake bite ranked as the second highest cause of child death in Thailand and nearby countries. Many other health institutions were begun in this way, including the tropical disease hospital in Ibadan, Nigeria, where there are what always seem to me like miles of children's wards.

THIRD WOMAN: I want to ask another question about the work of WHO. Can they really do anything about such tremendous health problems as, for example, tuberculosis in India?

FOURTH WOMAN: Yes! That's one of the diseases that used to be a "taken-for-granted" burden in many countries. Now many nations have had experience in preventing and controlling this disease and have been able to provide, through WHO and UNICEF, expert advice and technical assistance with the problem. It is a good example of how UN agencies work together. Thus the gradual hope for the total eradication of tuberculosis has been born; and the conquest of this disease is one of WHO's major, long-term commitments. It is based on two approaches: prevention, which involves large scale BCG vaccination campaigns (and in India this was undertaken and has already given protection to nearly sixty million people), and the treatment of tuberculosis sufferers, not only to cure them but to prevent the spread of further infection.

UNICEF has provided large quantities of BCG vaccine, tuberculin syringes, and vehicles for the biggest nationwide programs, such as in India. One of the essentials of a successful campaign against TB is the improvement of nutrition, especially among children. UNICEF has helped with children's nutrition and with emergency supplemental child feeding programs, as well as encouraging school and community gardens. Another UN specialized agency, the Food and Agriculture Organization, has also helped with nutrition education, with the development of milk production and conservation projects, and with substitutes for scarce vitamin- and protein-rich foods.

It is in the field of treatment WHO has, within the last few years, made the most remarkable advances. India, with its vast population, furnished the opportunity. They have an estimated two and one-half million active cases there—perhaps more. The worst part is that there are hospital beds for less than one per cent of these cases.

UN experts come from all over the world, you know, and so a WHO team headed by an English doctor started a project in Madras, South India. They wanted to discover whether patients given home treatment under careful supervision with the newest drugs might possibly do as well as those treated in hospitals. The results were most encouraging. Two years of experimentation demonstrated that patients treated at home under this system did, indeed, get well as rapidly as those in hospitals; and they had no recurrence of the disease. Equally important was the fact that their families remained uninfected.

How many millions of the world's population suffer from tuberculosis is not known. But the actual incidence of the disease has shown no dramatic increase. In the United States it has been a declining health menace for many years. And in recent years the number of deaths in an increasing number of countries has been virtually halved because of the discovery of new and easily administered drugs.

SECOND WOMAN: You mean that with all the health work our missionaries have done they haven't made more of an impression than that? It sounds like these new agencies are doing most of the real work.

FOURTH WOMAN: In our churches the problem has been that we haven't understood how great the need for work in health and other related fields really was. Because of this, we tended to feel smug about the comparatively infinitesimal contributions we have made toward the solution of these problems.

Please don't misunderstand me. The little we have been able to do has been very important. In many places the churches have built the first hospitals and trained the first medical personnel. This has been a wonderful contribution which gives newer, larger health programs something to build on. There are, however, several points I think we need to think about as we look at the world health situation and our mission work in that field.

First of all, we must be realistic about the size of the health problems of the world. Then we must see the comparative size of our mission programs. This is not to downgrade their importance. The money that we have given was well spent and has accomplished a great deal. But it is too bad that the people of the churches in the United States didn't put more money into missions, particularly during the time when their incomes were increasing.

FIRST WOMAN: I was looking at some figures the other day, and do you know we spend more for cosmetics or chewing gum and candy than we do for missions! You don't think it's too late for us to change this picture of ourselves, do you?

FOURTH WOMAN: Of course not! The next ten years may be crucial ones in many parts of the world. We could make a great contribution to the future of the world if we gave more money for mission programs through our Woman's Societies.

The most important thing for us to understand is that the need is gigantic. Every bit of assistance in solving those health problems is sorely needed. As church members we must increase our giving to meet this need. We have another responsibility also: as citizens we need to understand the work of organizations like WHO and UNICEF in which government has a responsibility.

SECOND WOMAN (*reluctantly*): I've learned a lot about the work that WHO, UNICEF, and other UN agencies are doing about the health problems around the world. I suppose it would be too much to hope that *we* get something out of it, too.

FOURTH WOMAN: Thank you for bringing me back to what I started to say originally. You remember we were discussing the fact that in our modern world, with its rapid transportation, disease anywhere is a danger to all of us. We considered two things we needed to do for our own good as well as that of others. The first was to deal with disease wherever it occurs. That is what we have just been talking about, and we benefit from it as well as do countries where disease is more widespread.

The second is to set up systems of protection against diseases that reach all nations. The World Health Organization has done an outstanding job on both of these.

One thing that would interest you, I think, is the

epidemic warning service. The League of Nations established this service, and the World Health Organization was formed in 1946 (through a request of the Economic and Social Council of the United Nations) to take over and enlarge the health work legacy that was received from the League of Nations.

In 1922 the League established centers in Moscow and Warsaw to report on the spread of disease, particularly typhus, which was then spreading disaster across postwar Europe, particularly among the destitute and starving peoples of Eastern Europe. Today this epidemic warning service is operated by the World Health Organization and is called Epidnations. Its radio system transmits daily radio bulletins from Geneva which carry urgent information to the whole world on dangerous epidemic diseases. The Weekly Epidemiological Record is a printed document which presents a fuller, less hurried picture. There is even a monthly service that is more analytical and complete.

One of the best examples of how this system works was demonstrated by the serious cholera epidemic that broke out in Egypt in 1947. This dread disease, for hundreds of years one of the greatest killers of mankind, broke out intensely in the Suez region and spread rapidly through most of Egypt. The Epidnations warning system announced the epidemic to the world within a few hours of its confirmation.

WHO began collecting as large a supply of cholera vaccine as possible for the Egyptian government. The United States, Russia, India, and many other countries rushed in supplies. WHO held an emergency commission meeting in Geneva where the epidemic was discussed by many kinds of experts. Their report indicated that the disease could be confined inside Egypt if the established provisions of the international sanitary conditions were observed. This meant, among other things, limitation of nonessential travel to and from Egypt and vaccinations of people crossing borders.

The disease did not spread, and the world had a dramatic demonstration of how cooperation can protect us all. This made it easier for WHO to get agreements from member countries on necessary precautions and regulations. The daily bulletins broadcast by WHO forewarned authorities at ports and airfields so that special precautions could be observed when necessary.

I'm sure that several of you, when you were traveling abroad, have had a yellow health card on which your doctor recorded the inoculations or vaccinations that he gave you. That is known around the world as the World Health Card. Remember how carefully it was examined by health authorities whenever you entered a country, including your own? That card constituted protection for you and for those with whom you associated abroad (and for a few weeks after your return home). Your doctor knew what shots you needed before you began your trip because of the world health reports. Doctors who examined your World Health Card along the way knew what emergency measures might need to be taken when you encountered unexpected epidemics.

There are other less dramatic health services which help us in the United States. WHO has prepared a worldwide pharmacopoeia which gives standards for all recognized drugs. This is of great help when you need a prescription filled in foreign countries. There is a WHO chemical reference center in Stockholm that helps doctors to classify dangerous and complex disease agents when new health problems arise in their countries.

Certain services essential to the maintenance of world health can only be provided on a global basis. Warnings of disease, emergency assistance, and expert advice are among these. In the same way, worldwide standards of strength and purity of drugs, internationally agreed upon quarantine regulations, and the design of disease control campaigns for individual governments are best performed by a world organization of this type.

I never cease to be grateful for the two ways in which the UN helps to protect the health of my family and me, as well as to help other lands begin the long battle against controllable disease.

RESOURCES

ORDER THE FOLLOWING FROM THE SERVICE CENTER
7820 READING ROAD, CINCINNATI, OHIO 45237

United Nations and Women. By Margaret R. Bender. This study guide prepared especially for use in the units of the World Federation of Methodist Women explains what the United Nations is, what it does, how it can help you and you can help it. Written in an easy and popular style and generously illustrated. 25 cents.

The United Nations and Our Children's World. Ways that families can learn more about the UN. Free.

What's Going On Here? A United Nations sampler. Free.

The Methodist Office at the Church Center for the United Nations. Pictorial leaflet describing the functions of this office. 15 cents each; 4 for 50 cents.

A New United Nations for a New World. Leaflet on the changing role of the United Nations. Free.

For pamphlets, films, filmstrips, and other publications available, write for catalogs from:

United States Committee for UNICEF
P. O. Box 1618
Church Street Station
New York, N.Y. 10008

World Health Organization
WHO Regional Office
Public Information Office
1501 New Hampshire Avenue, N.W.
Washington, D.C.

ORDER THE FOLLOWING FROM THE WRIGHT STUDIO
5264 BROOKVILLE ROAD, INDIANAPOLIS, INDIANA 46219

World Flags Centerpiece (see "The World Our Parish") $1.50

New Nations Flags Centerpiece. A companion to the World Flags Centerpiece. $1.50

New Nations Puzzlemat. An intriguing maze leads the user from one to another interesting fact about some of the baffling problems that confront new nations as they seek to make real their dreams of freedom. 20 for 75 cents.

Global Seals Kit. 30 gummed Global Seals, colored paper for making 10 unusual discussion-stimulating favors, plus an Idea Sheet for many other clever favors made of Seals. Per kit, 30 cents.

Global Napkin. (see "'Opportunity to Study")

Eighty-four Small Flags. Printed in full color on both sides. Cut apart for making of games, favors, maps, etc. Per sheet, 45 cents.

Creative Uses for New Nations Accessories. Extremely helpful ideas for dinners, special occasions, and general uses of the accessories. 15 cents.

UN Flags. Cut apart and mount on toothpicks or soda straws for individual favors. 2¼ x 2½ inches. 2 cents each.

ABOUT THE AUTHOR

Mrs. Clifford A. Bender (Margaret Rigg) is executive secretary in the Section of Christian Social Relations with special responsibility in the field of international affairs. She represents the Board of Missions as official observer at the United Nations. She is one of the two executives in charge of the Church Center for the United Nations—an office jointly maintained by the Board of Christian Social Concerns and by the Section of Christian Social Relations of the Woman's Division.

Mrs. Bender was born in Woodbine, Iowa, and grew up in Seattle, Washington. She has an M.A. degree from the University of Washington in Seattle and did additional graduate work at Uppsala, Sweden, as a Fellow of the American Scandinavian Foundation. She has also done graduate work at Columbia University.

Mrs. Bender is an ardent champion of the United Nations, particularly of its Commission on the Status of Women. Last year she represented the Commission of the Churches on International Affairs at the 18th session of the UN Commission of the Status of Women in Teheran, Iran. In the past, Mrs. Bender has visited many lands and observed not only the projects of the Board of Missions of The Methodist Church but also United Nations work, particularly that of UNICEF.

Metamorphosis of a Circle

Editor's Note: The following is based on the experience of the Evening Circle of the Woman's Society of Christian Service of the Leonia Methodist Church, Leonia, New Jersey. The narrative material was compiled and written by Shirley and Leonard Perryman.* The program "How it Feels To Be Black in White America" was prepared by Mrs. Philip Y. Paterson and Mrs. Gregory M. Ricciardi. Other programs referred to were researched and prepared by various circle members.

Most of the twenty members of our Evening Circle have some measure of higher education. We have young children and are involved in school activities, fund drives, church, school, bridge clubs, Scouts, etc. A number of us are wives of executives of the Board of Missions. Many of our husbands commute to New York. Perhaps we have more resources for speakers and other interesting programs than some groups. In short, we are typical women in a typical Methodist church in a typical white suburban community doing typical things.

We, as Christian women, do not yet fully understand nor do we know what our roles should be in the midst of the social and political changes in the world about us. We had long sought speakers to bring us programs on subjects of interest but we knew we had not been searching within ourselves to find the role of the attitudes which we, as Christian women, must have if we are to face a dynamic, changing society and guide our children as they mature in a world so different from that in which we grew up.

We gradually became aware that we must change our pattern of programs. Our change did not come rapidly but emerged over a three-year period.

---

* Leonard Perryman is director of the Department of News Service, Methodist Board of Missions, and his wife Shirley finds her place in a local society.

We first explored various study books which really challenged us to think beyond ourselves. The book *Who Cares*, by Jeanette T. Harrington and Muriel S. Webb (Friendship Press, New York, $1.70), laid bare this challenge before us. As we viewed the film *A Moment to Act* (produced by the National Council of Churches, Broadcasting and Film Commission, 1962, rental $8.00), which accompanied this study, we all knew we did care and must in some manner become involved in something beyond ourselves.

Our first decision was to participate in an actual project of help. For this we chose to contribute $10.00 a month for one year through MCOR (Methodist Committee for Overseas Relief) for relief work with Korean war orphans at Angel's Haven, a Methodist home in Seoul. (This was over and above our pledges to the Woman's Society.) Next was a program of study based on Huston Smith's book *Religions of Man*, illustrated by filmstrips and produced by *Life* magazine. (Harper paperback, 85 cents.) This challenged us to ask ourselves, "Why are we Christians? Is it really necessary to carry the Christian message to other people with different beliefs?" But more important was the question, "What is our Christian responsibility in this changing world? What is the nature of this changing world?"

In the third year our changed emphasis in programing came to a focus. After much discussion, two areas of social ferment seemed to demand that we explore them because we knew and understood them least. The first was the Negro freedom movement; the second, the meaning of poverty in a time of overwhelming affluence.

We were reading of Negro demonstrations, civil rights bills, demands for equal housing, desegregated facilities, equal employment, . . . dignity. We read what the white man wrote, but this did not make us understand this tremendous movement. Thus our first program was in the field of literature so that we might know how it feels to be black in white America. For only as we read what the Negro had written could we begin to grasp his feelings, ambitions, attitudes, hopes, and desires in relation to his role in society.

Next the question arose as to the Negro's role in past society or history. Our standard textbooks told us little, if anything, beyond his importation as slave labor, his emancipation, and about the careers of a very few men such as Booker T. Washington. Our second program was, therefore, one on the history of the Negro not only in the United States but in African civilization.

It was at this point that our third program came into being. How should we feel toward people from whom we have traditionally been separated? Each of us had been challenged to consider the question of the Negro in society in a manner which we had heretofore neglected. And ultimately, we hope we have come to a new understanding of our Christian responsibility in the area of race relations.

Poverty to most of us seemed to be the shack dweller, the slum victim, the Skid Row resident, the unemployed, the destitute elderly person, or the many other persons who lived in degrading circumstances. How could we equate poverty with persons who did have an income or who could work if they only would, did have a TV, did have a car, did have a roof over their heads, food for their tables or clothes on their backs, and who were not on relief rolls? We all knew what it was like not to be able to buy everything we wanted and to run short of funds at times. Why shouldn't these people just work harder, save more, and quit whining? Or why didn't the man without a job just go out and get one? Wouldn't our husbands do that?

But as we began to think seriously about what it means to earn a minimal income in a time of high employment, to lack needed skills, to lose one's job because your service is no longer needed, or to find a machine can do what you and several of your co-workers used to do, then we began to grasp a new understanding of the word "poverty." We began to understand what poverty does to a person, not only economically, but what it does emotionally to him and to his family.

Our final program of our year was what we called a "Symbolic Sacrificial Supper." This was to try to understand what it would be like to be one of the poor of our nation or of the world. We found how to eat cheaply, but not poorly, for we certainly had a nutritionally well-balanced meal. It pointed out to us how difficult it is for us with our education, advantages, and economic well-being to understand truly the problems of the poor.

We have felt a challenge to use our advantages to help others. Perhaps it will be only the contribution of funds to worthy agencies; perhaps it will be helping boys and girls, whether poor or affluent, to develop to their fullest so they may not feel the degradation of poverty.

In addition to our two main program thrusts, the Negro freedom movement and the affluence-poverty dilemma, we did not neglect other areas of our concern as Methodist women. We looked at the critical problem of church-state relationships from the historical and contemporary perspectives. We used the Spiritual Life Study Book on Genesis as one program, and we considered our part in the Christian mission in Latin America through a report on an evangelistic visit to Peru and other Latin American countries by our pastor (one of the evangelistic missions sponsored jointly by the Board of Evangelism and the Board of Missions). As an outgrowth of this last report and our poverty study, the circle gave, over and above their pledges, $120 which was matched by funds from the total church to the Peoples Institute of Rio de Janeiro, Brazil.

This, in brief, is where we have come thus far as a Circle in a changing world. However, this is not the end of our metamorphosis, and it may never be complete.

January 1965—At the Saturday "coffee" the group was very congenial. One woman, who worked during the day, said, "I think this kind of meeting is good because we have a real reason for coming together" (deciding how to use the bazaar money). Another business woman said, "I refuse to go to monthly meetings and just listen to reports." This gave us some clues as to what the women would respond to.

In such a city church as ours most of the women have many social contacts outside the church and do not need the Woman's Society of Christian Service socially. (By this time most of the elderly core group has passed away or were too infirm to get out much.) Many women have jobs during the day, and those who don't, have young children at home to be cared for. There are not enough women to think of forming a Woman's Society of Christian Service and a Wesleyan Service Guild. There are very few with grown children and lots of time. One of the projects decided upon at the coffee meeting was to continue the traditional Colonial Dinner.

February 1965—The Colonial Dinner put on by the women (but assisted by total church) raised about two hundred dollars; half was given to Interfaith Neighbors and half to the church.

May 1965—A tour to Church of All Nations was planned and given ample publicity—five women and the pastor attended.

The pastor felt something must be done and planned a spring luncheon for June. He asked me to chair the Women's Group (we were very afraid to use the name Woman's Society of Christian Service for fear it would kill any program). Volunteers agreed to serve as secretary, treasurer and bazaar chairman. We called together a group of women who, we thought, would have creative ideas. They thought a service project would be good to unite the whole group.

June 1965—At the luncheon one of the former officers, a

professional church worker, gave a most inspiring talk. About fifty women attended.

August 1965—A nearby Children's Shelter, which we thought would be an ideal service project, said they did not need any help. We really wondered what kind of "programs" to plan. One of the planners had been president in the days when most of the members were elderly. She said, "The ladies loved to go to the District Meetings. I would take a carload, and we had six ladies at all those meetings. For most of them it was their only outing and social event. Now many of those ladies have passed away."

September 1965—Officers, the member who looked into the service project, and the pastor met in my home to plan a program to be presented at the next luncheon. We decided to mimeograph a Calendar of Events listing local and district meetings of the Woman's Society of Christian Service and events in the community of which our women would want to be aware, such as Union Seminary courses. Women were asked to "talk-up" each event and make telephone calls. Coffee hour group leaders would play an essential part in publicizing the coming events to their group. (This sounds like circles, but these groups have a definite purpose to serve coffee after church, and they respond to this.) Each group leader has been asked by the minister to let him know of any pastoral concerns and to keep in touch with her group. Possibly two groups will meet together socially or for some project this year.

The second part of the booklet will be an extensive listing of community volunteer opportunities in which the women may take part. Since there is no one service project, we will encourage wide participation in many projects; and possibly the volunteers will want to come together to discuss their service in terms of their Christian faith and receive inspiration and encouragement from each other and the minister.

Fall Luncheon—As each person came in, I tried to greet

her personally. I felt hypocritical in a way; maybe I should explain.

I feel that women should be coming out to church functions because they feel the church has a job to do for the world, and, hopefully, that the function is essential to that mission. However, to be realistic, most women come out only if they "want to" or "feel like it" at the moment; a personal invitation from the pastor or president makes them feel wanted, and they are more likely to attend. It is still upsetting to me to have to play such a social role.

I forgot to mention, we had thirty-three women, far more than we had food for! I told the group that we had debated as to whether we should call ourselves the Woman's Society of Christian Service, but upon defining its real purpose, it was also the purpose of our group. We had four officers, a bazaar chairman, and an executive planning committee (composed of former officers). I said, "The word 'Christian' separates us from the Garden Club, the Women's Club, the Parents' Association and the Hospital Auxiliary. Because we come here as Christian women, we have the blessings and purposes which are embodied in our faith; and just as we are distinct, we must try to avoid duplicating or imitating those groups which are devoted to other specific secular purposes. We are special." I'm not keen on the bazaar, but it's successful and is a way that our women like to work together, and it makes money! To placate my conscience I said, "Most Woman's Societies advise their members to pledge a certain amount to make up their budget. We are not asking this of you. But we are asking for you to take part in the bazaar. This is where your stewardship comes in."

October 1965—The women's group (I feel we now can and should call ourselves the Woman's Society of Christian Service as we are in agreement with the principles, if not the practices, of this group) sponsored a study series on a current and meaningful book, *The Secular City,* by Harvey Cox.

Early in the month we got a group of five women together to plan for the study. This was to be a church-wide study, and although the Woman's Society was sponsoring it and helping to supplement the cost of books, we did not publicize our backing because we did not want to drive men away. Also, one of the most dynamic women of our church would not be a member of the Society but was willing to take part in the challenge offered by the study. The average attendance (which always seems to be so important to Methodists) was about nineteen for four Sunday sessions. Men and women attended. Several couples promised to continue discussions in their homes.

On Saturday, October 30, about twenty-five women came together to plan for the bazaar. Everyone volunteered to take some job. However, as far as outside volunteer activities go, I don't think anyone has reached out!

October 7, 1965—Along with five other women from the Woman's Society of Christian Service, I attended the district meeting. The morning speaker was well known, but I felt she was "coddling" the "old gals." Maybe it's better not to "shake them up," but as long as the Woman's Society of Christian Service is not presenting a vital and up-to-date program, I doubt whether it will attract young women who aren't impressed by the old myths, stereotypes, and lack of involvement of former days. The afternoon speakers were from Methodist agencies, Church of All Nations, Methodist Home; so at least they were interesting in content.

One of the morning hymns was paraphrased so that one verse went "let washing, cleaning, making beds not simply chores each woman dreads, but acts of devotion, etc.," (this is not an exact quote; but until we learn to stop deifying household work, we will never emancipate the housewife and enable her to be creative as a Christian).

I estimated that besides myself there were possibly only four others under forty years old in the whole group. P.S. The other women from my church thought the meeting was "inspiring."

November 1965—A "remnant or core group" (four to be exact) financed their own weekend trip to Washington, D.C., to visit the Church of the Saviour which has a unique fellowship and ministry in that city. Part of the incentive in our going rests on our concern for renewal in the local church and the responsibility we feel for understanding what it means to be called to mission. We are convinced that the pattern of the Church of the Saviour cannot be copied in our situation, but it does say something to us about the meaning of commitment.

We have plans until January, at which time we will plan the spring program. This allows time to assess the response to the earlier programs. I would like to see the Woman's Society of Christian Service sponsor a weekend retreat in late winter or early spring to talk about the meaning of renewal in the Christian's personal and corporate life.

As I reflect on our plans, it seems we are devoted to study and service. Through these channels we can provide additional dimensions to our local church.

The question is, will our women respond to this loose organizational form and to individually rendered services?

. . . .

Some questions to consider as you strive to determine your own pattern, one that fits your particular situation, yet one which keeps you aware of the needs of the world and the church's mission in the world, are listed below. Hopefully, others will come to mind as the reader prepares her program; but these are listed to assure partici-

ORGANIZED FOR ACTION

pants that, while this society is having its struggles, it is not "bucking the system" just to be naughty.

1. What does the Woman's Society offer that is not to be found in the commissions?

2. Can the Society reach some women who are not active in the commissions?

3. In the interest of renewal in the church and a genuine search for new and meaningful patterns, how free can a local group be to struggle, through trial and error, for patterns to fit its needs?

4. How can persons be led to form new concepts of mission in the world through active interest in needs of their own community?

5. What are the dimensions of a bazaar—its preparation and its actual execution—that have value for the total church? Other than financial?

6. How can a group in search of its own patterns utilize the dichotomy of struggle to enrich and enlarge the religious life of the total church even as it recognizes the need to be a part of a "connectional system"?

7. How does such a group not just give an annual contribution to missions but help its members know and understand the mission and want to make personal pledges toward its support?

The Giver and the Receiver

MAYNARD SHELLY

GIVER (*holding something in a brown paper sack*): I brought something for you.

RECEIVER: What is it?

GIVER (*still holding sack*): Oh, it's just a pie.

RECEIVER: It is? Why?

GIVER (*s.h.s.*): Well, I just thought you'd like to have a pie. So I brought you one.

RECEIVER: That's nice—I guess. And I guess I should just take it and say thank you. But why be cut and dried? I wonder if we might not talk about this pie just a bit?

GIVER (*s.h.s.*): You don't like my pies?

RECEIVER: Frankly, I've had better. But that's not the point. Even if your pie were a good pie, I wonder why you want to give me a pie?

GIVER (*s.h.s.*): I just felt I ought to help you over this rough spot. You have your troubles. And besides you are always helping people too.

RECEIVER: This is a way of paying me back?

GIVER (*s.h.s.*): That's putting it rather bluntly.

RECEIVER: Well, shall we say you feel indebted to me and since you would rather have me indebted to you than you be indebted to me, you're trying to get ahead of me?

GIVER (*s.h.s.*): You've said it again, but I don't understand you quite as well.

RECEIVER: I liked it better the other way.

GIVER (*s.h.s.*): Are you trying to infer that I'm trying to better myself by giving you this pie?

RECEIVER: Yes, I sure am. The moral of our little conversation is just this: Your need to give is bigger than my need to receive.

GIVER (*s.h.s.*): It is?

RECEIVER: Yes. Even though my children are sick, the water has been shut off by the water company, I got my last unemployment check last month, and we haven't had bread for two days—the answer is still yes.

GIVER (*s.h.s.*): For a hungry person, you're sure philosophical.

RECEIVER: It helps to be hungry.

GIVER (*s.h.s.*): You don't think it is wrong for me to be giving you this pie?

RECEIVER: Certainly not, and especially not if it's rhubarb.

GIVER (*s.h.s.*): Well, let's see how did this pie idea come to me? Oh, yes, I just noticed that we had two pies and then I remembered that you probably had none. It just didn't seem right.

RECEIVER: You felt guilty about having so many pies? If you give me one, you won't feel so guilty about still having one pie plus one cake, three boxes of assorted crackers and cookies, a gallon of ice cream, and an icebox full of leftovers?

GIVER (*s.h.s.*): You're drooling on the sack.

RECEIVER: You're avoiding the question.

GIVER (*s.h.s.*): You're not my psychiatrist, either.

RECEIVER: Sorry.

GIVER (*s.h.s.*): Don't you believe it's more blessed to give than to receive? That's what it says in the Bible. Acts 20:35.

RECEIVER: Perhaps so, but we receivers need a lot of grace. It's not easy to take all this stuff and keep your self-respect. But it helps me to remember that I'm giving you givers something by taking what you offer.

GIVER (*s.h.s.*): You'll take the pie?

RECEIVER: Did you ever doubt it? But let's go one more round.

GIVER (*s.h.s.*): The pie is getting heavy.

RECEIVER: I suspect that you want me to come to your church.

GIVER (*s.h.s.*): Well, yes.

RECEIVER: I don't know whether I like being bribed with a crummy old pie.

GIVER (*s.h.s.*): It's cherry.

RECEIVER: That's the best kind of a bribe, except for rhubarb.

GIVER (*s.h.s.*): Sure, I want you to come to our church. But whether you ever do or not, I want to give you this pie.

RECEIVER: I like you. You're kind of honest.

GIVER (*s.h.s.*): You've driven me to it.

RECEIVER: You've made me feel like somebody. Not just a pie-taker.

GIVER (*holding out the sack*): Can I ask you to do something for me? Next time—

RECEIVER (*taking the brown paper sack*): Yes?

GIVER: Just say thank you and shut up.

Reprinted by permission from *The Mennonite*.

A BRIEF HISTORICAL SKETCH OF THE WOMAN'S SOCIETY OF CHRISTIAN SERVICE AND THE WESLEYAN SERVICE GUILD.*

The Methodist Church sprang from the Church of England. It began with the "heartwarming" experience of John Wesley in the eighteenth century. Though English in origin, the American branch started by Francis Asbury has spread almost around the world.

THE METHODIST WOMAN'S SOCIETIES

The first church-wide Methodist Woman's Society was founded in 1869 in Boston, Massachusetts, in response to an urgent call from the wives of two missionaries in India. From their own experiences, these two women made it abundantly clear that there was a serious need for unmarried missionaries in India. After the Civil War, women's work in the Sanitary Commissions and similar agencies of mercy to soldiers was ended; they were eager for a compelling new interest. This "new interest" became the "Woman's Foreign Missionary Society" of the Methodist Episcopal Church. Small and feeble and ridiculed by masculine leaders, the local group in Boston branched out until it became an important element in the rapidly developing "woman's movement" of the period.

Its evangelical message started in India, but gradually spread into other areas. To the astonishment of its critics and in spite of a rather naïve lack of centralization, its eleven groups were, by common zeal and loyalty, welded into an unexpectedly efficient working system. Each branch embraced several conference societies, and each had a treasurer who sent remittances directly to the

---

* This sketch is adapted from material prepared by Miss Florence Hooper that was included in a program for the Women of the Evangelical United Brethren Church about the Woman's Society of Christian Service.

ORGANIZED FOR ACTION

foreign fields. One high-placed gentleman called the complex a "hydra-headed monster." Yet there emerged essential unity of administration through a General Executive Committee that represented all branches and guided the whole.

The "brethren" of that Victorian era advised, "You raise the money; we will administer it." But the women held firmly to their purpose, handled their own funds, and despite its very real clumsiness, developed a system that one progressive masculine authority declared was as efficient in the Orient as the Standard Oil Company.

At the same time here at home, there were glaring needs for schools for the American Indians, schools for children of the newly emancipated Negroes, for settlement houses in large cities, and other welfare projects. In 1880, the Woman's Home Missionary Society of the Methodist Episcopal Church was created to help solve American social problems.

Later, the Wesleyan Service Guild grew out of business and professional women's groups who were interested in both home and foreign missions. It was part of both the parent organizations. Its growth was evidence of an increasing host of Christian business women whose influence in church and community was becoming an undreamed of importance.

Meanwhile, in the Methodist Episcopal Church, South, urgent appeals for help for women in China led to the formation in 1873 of the "Women's Bible Mission at Home and Abroad," based in Baltimore. Later, generous donors in Nashville and elsewhere founded a girls' school in Shanghai that became famous in the China Mission. In 1878, these efforts coalesced into a "Woman's Board of Foreign Missions." Home missions work was organized "almost entirely because of one inspired woman, Miss Lucinda B. Helm." Later these boards merged to form the Woman's Council, an organic part of the Board of Missions of the Methodist Episcopal Church, South.

ORGANIZED FOR ACTION

The third group, the Methodist Protestant Church, organized its "Woman's Foreign Missionary Society" in 1879 in response to the pleas of a missionary from Japan. Out of this Society's annual meeting in 1893 grew the "Woman's Home Missionary Society" devoted to work among Kentucky mountain people, city missions, a children's home, and a lodge for business girls. In 1928, all the missionary and educational concerns of the Methodist Protestant Church merged into one "Board of Missions."

When the three churches united in 1940, harmonizing such diverse organizations into a new all-embracing Woman's Society of Christian Service was a major problem. Beside the missionary groups, in practically every church there was a "Ladies' Aid" devoted to parish matters, care of parsonages, and church housekeeping. About that time, these Ladies' Aids seriously considered forming a national society. However, as unification neared, this idea was dropped until the merging of Ladies' Aids into the Woman's Society of Christian Service could be considered in connection with an already complicated situation.

THE WOMAN'S SOCIETY OF CHRISTIAN SERVICE

But in 1940 the new Woman's Society of Christian Service was formed, and its Woman's Division became an autonomous part of the Board of Missions of The Methodist Church. Unification of fiercely possessive groups, working under different plans in relation to the denominations as a whole, with varying interests—some nationwide, some worldwide, some parochial in outreach—was a real miracle of grace. Time, experience, and the operation of that sweet reasonableness of which we all have at least a modicum, have wrought a true personality. The Division has prospered financially and increased in membership. In the United States and its territories, it has been associated with over three hundred institutions. It has reached into forty-five countries overseas. Many of its endeavors are in cooperation with other denominations.

Through the Department of Christian Social Relations it has influenced major areas of social concern. The Charter of Racial Policies of the Woman's Division was a milestone in this area. "World Understanding" emphasis has found expression in nationwide workshops. A half million dollar appropriation from the Division helped underwrite the Church Center for the United Nations in New York City.

The Division has used its resources of money and personnel to meet the intensified demands for literature and literacy throughout the world. They have had their own programs and also contributed through the Committee on World Literacy and Christian Literature.

1964 REORGANIZATION

Today reveals new potential for wider growth; new challenge for greater efficiency; new calls for creative change. In September 1964 a reorganization of the Board of Missions took place. No major changes in organization of the Woman's Society of Christian Service at local levels are involved, however, except somewhat different names for certain offices, integration of work for children and youth into the program of the local congregation as a whole. Local, district and conference Woman's Societies of Christian Service function as before, raising their own funds and remitting them, through the usual channels, to the newly structured Woman's Division in New York.

Funds remitted from the local Societies are used in all parts of the Board of Missions according to the vote of the Woman's Division. Requests for the use of this money come from the other units of the Board which have responsibility for administering institutions and programs in the United States and overseas.

The new features are incorporated in the 1965 Constitution of the Woman's Division. The Board of Mis-

ORGANIZED FOR ACTION

sions consists of a World Division, a National Division, and a Woman's Division. The administration of all home and foreign institutions is within the National and World Divisions. The Woman's Society and Guild still have responsibility for education, interpretation, and support of these institutions. The divisions may make by-laws in harmony with the constitution and charter of the Board and, with its approval, each will develop and carry out its assigned function.

The Joint Commission on Education and Cultivation, and the Joint Committee on Missionary Personnel serve all three divisions.

The 1965 Report of the Board of Missions carries a chart explaining in full the organizational pattern of the Board. (See Additional Resource List.)

To the Woman's Division is entrusted the interpretation of the mission of Christ and his church as stated in the "Purpose" of the Woman's Society of Christian Service and the Wesleyan Service Guild.

ADDITIONAL RESOURCES

ORDER THE FOLLOWING FROM THE SERVICE CENTER
7820 READING ROAD, CINCINNATI, OHIO 45237

Service Center Catalog, Board of Missions, The Methodist Church (Free)

A Handbook for the Woman's Society of Christian Service. Basic information on the total work and outreach of the local society. (50 cents)

Constitution and By-Laws, 1965 edition Constitution and By-Laws of the Woman's Division, Woman's Society of Christian Service, Wesleyan Service Guild, Board of Missions of The Methodist Church. (60 cents)

Handbook on Program. The work of the Program Committee and of all lines of work related to it. (50 cents)

Handbook on Finance. The financial policies and goals of the Woman's Society of Christian Service. (50 cents)

Handbook for the Wesleyan Service Guild (50 cents)

The Annual Report of The Board of Missions of The Methodist Church ($1.50)

Handbook—World Federation of Methodist Women. A brief history of the Federation; list of areas and units; list of officers; names and addresses of official correspondents of all units. (50 cents)

Prayer Calendar. Booklet offering daily guidance in prayer so that every worker and all the work of the Board of Missions may be offered for prayer during the year. Names, addresses, birthday of active missionaries and deaconesses given. (60 cents)

The Methodist Woman, monthly magazine containing helpful material for local Woman's Societies of Christian Service. Annual subscription ($1.50)

World Outlook, monthly magazine; information about mission of The Methodist Church; projects, program emphases, etc. Annual subscription ($2.00)

Combination subscriptions for both magazines ($3.30)

Methodists Missions at a Glance. Survey with world map **(Free)**

Order the following from the Cokesbury Store nearest you:

The Methodist Hymnal

The Book of Worship

These two volumes provide material which will prove invaluable in planning and participating in more worshipful experiences. (Prices quoted from your nearest Cokesbury Store)

Audiovisuals

(Catalog) **A Comprehensive List of Audio-Visual Materials**, recommended by the general boards and agencies for use in Methodist churches. This also contains a listing of Conference and Area Audiovisual Libraries, Regional Service Centers, and Cokesbury Stores who can supply audiovisual materials, and the Methodist Boards and Agencies who distribute them. This List was a special supplement of **The Methodist Story** which every Methodist pastor received. Consult your local pastor for this information.

The following are suggested as being suitable supplementary material for the programs in this book.

Who Am I? Who Are You? Who Are We?:

"Members One of Another"—color filmstrip with reading script. Deals with the subject of interpersonal relationships. For sale from Cokesbury, $5.50. For rent, check conference film library.

United With Women Everywhere:

"Maramba of Rhodesia"—color, 15 min. film. A day in the life of a young boy in an African village seen through his eyes; showing his relationships to his mother, father, friends. Rental from Cokesbury $5.00.

"New Faces of Africa"—b&w or color, 28 min. film. Showing the old and new Africa existing side by side; describing bonds of unity among Africans. Documents the way African Christians witness to their faith in times of change. Rental from Cokesbury, $8.00, b&w; $12.00, color. Ask for leader's guide.

ORGANIZED FOR ACTION

The World Our Parish:

"The Day Geography Got Lost"*—b&w, 30 min. film. Produced for the Methodist Youth Fund. Illustrates the interrelatedness of Christians everywhere. Shows how a youth group in the U.S.A. receives a gift and a surprise from a youth group in Sarawak. Rental from Cokesbury, $7.00.

"Return by Sea"—color, 28 min. film. A missionary's son, now a Navy chaplain, returns to the Philippines where he grew up and tells of advances in Christian outreach. Rental from Cokesbury, $8.00.

"Women from Southern Asia"—color, sound filmstrip. Tells the story of Christian women in India and Pakistan and their links with Methodist women in America. Sale from Service Center, $5.00.

"Where the Atom is Split":

"Household of Faith"—b&w or color, 30 min. film. A documentary showing churches working cooperatively, stressing the need for all churches to be "sending" and "receiving" churches. Rental from Cokesbury, b&w, $8.00; color, $12.00.

"A Foundation for Dialogue"—Two-color sound filmstrip; 209 frames, 43 min., with a 12" 33⅓ rpm record. For youth and adults. Survey of the major Christian denominations in contemporary America. This initial understanding of the life, faith, and worship of other Christians provides a sound basis for positive thinking in the area of ecumenism and Christian dialogue. $8.50. Order from the Convent of St. Catherine, Racine, Wisconsin 53402.

"Pakistan Report"—color sound filmstrip, 15 min. narration on 33⅓ rpm record, script, guide. Report on Methodist work in Pakistan: city, village and desert. Sale from Service Center $5.00.

"The World in a Word" *—color, filmstrip, with script. Art plus a thought-provoking script define the word "ecumenical" in terms of its meaning in people's lives. Sale from Service Center $6.00.

---

* This film might be used in conjunction with an all-church affair, or be presented jointly with the Methodist Youth Fellowship.

ORGANIZED FOR ACTION

For All Who Stumble:

"Heart of the Neighborhood"—b&w or color, 29 min. film. Shows the influence of Marcy Center in Chicago on the lives of youth and families. Rental from Cokesbury, $8.00, color; $4.00, b&w.

What It Feels Like to Be a Negro in White America:

"The Broken Mask"—b&w or color, 29 min. film. The friendship between a Negro boy and a white, which began at a church camp, runs into difficulty when they go to a local church. Rental from Cokesbury, b&w, $8.00; color, $12.00.

"No Man Is an Island"—b&w, 26 min. film. Two friends, one Negro and one white, face the prejudices of their community. From the CBS-TV "Look Up and Live" series. Ask for guide. Rental from Cokesbury $6.50.

"The New Girl"—b&w, 31 min. film. Dramatization of experiences of a Negro girl at the time a company extends an Equal Job Opportunity Policy to its office staff. Rental from Cokesbury, $5.00.

"It Happens Every Day"—color filmstrip with reading script. Using symbolism, this points beyond racial similarities and differences to the common denominator of humanity. Sale from Service Center, $5.00.

"An Inclusive Church"—color sound filmstrip. Presentation of the Central Jurisdiction, its problems and special relationships to the other Jurisdictions of The Methodist Church. It outlines strengths and weaknesses which must be considered as a merger of the Central Jurisdiction with the geographic jurisdictions is contemplated. Sale from Service Center, $10.

"The Woman on Center Street." (A play) A dramatic presentation on the Charter of Racial Policies. 50 cents each; 4 for $1.50.

"Adventures in Negro History." 38⅓ rpm record. Highlights of Negro contributions from pre-Colonial times to today's Space Age. $1.00 and 3 Pepsi corks. Pepsi-Cola Company, Box 134, New York, N.Y. 10046.

In Dialogue with Women of Southeast Asia:

"Witnesses Together"—color, 25 min. film. Produced by the East Asia Christian Conference, done in Asia by Asian Christians to show the purpose and outreach of the East Asia Christian Conference, an organization related to American churches. Rental from Cokesbury, $8.00.

Conversations in Poverty:

"How Things Hide People"—color filmstrip with record. Presentation of persons who live in affluent culture, difficulties they experience in grasping reality of poverty. Sale from Service Center, $7.50.

"The Stepsitters"—b&w 25 min. film. Produced by the Methodist Youth Fund. Dramatic documentary tells how skill and patience win over a gang of boys at the Homer Toberman Settlement House. Rental from Cokesbury, $5.00.

Opportunity to Study:

"Portrait of a Woman"—color film produced for the 25th Anniversary of the Woman's Society of Christian Service. A documentary emphasizing the continuing need to support the education of women around the world. Filmed in Brazil, Korea and Africa. Rental from Cokesbury, $5.00.

"South of the Clouda"—b&w 36 min. film. The story of a wealthy Muslim girl who meets new ways of thinking at the Christian college in Beirut, Lebanon. Rental from Cokesbury, $6.00.

"We Receive to Give"—color sound filmstrip with 33⅓ rpm record. Depicts, through lives of graduates of educational institutions supported by Methodist women, the Christian influence of these schools. Sale from Service Center, $5.00.

Focus on World Health—The Church and the United Nations:

"Miracle in Java"—b&w 29 min. film. Shows how a doctor in Indonesia, with the help of UN agencies and specialists, organized his country's first rehabilitation center for crippled and limbless children and adults; narrated by Edward R. Murrow. Rental from: Contemporary Films, 267 W. 25th Street, New York, N.Y. 10001, $7.50.

"Overture"—b&w 9 min. film. Performance of Beethoven's Egmont Overture illustrated by scenes showing the effect of war and UN efforts to aid in reconstruction, peace. Effective in creating mood for worship. Rental from Cokesbury, $4.00.

"World Without End"—b&w 45 min. film. Shows how people of the world, no matter where they live, are faced with similar problems and how the United Nations is working to help them attain a peaceful, healthy, prosperous community of nations. Rental from: Brandon Films, Inc., 200 W. 57th Street, New York, N.Y. 10019, $7.50.

"For the Healing of the Nations"—color, 10 min. filmstrip with 33⅓ rpm record and guide. Shows the development of the Church Center for the United Nations; from earliest stages until completion. Purpose and service of the Center are carefully interpreted. Major contribution for this building made by Methodist women. Sale, Service Center, $5.00.

"Let There Be Life"—b&w filmstrip, captioned. Shows how UN agencies like World Health Organization and the United Nations Children's Fund are at work around the world. Sale from Cokesbury, $3.00.

Please Note:

Regarding **Free** materials from the Service Center: Materials are **free** for single copies. In quantity there is a nominal charge for handling and postage—25 copies, 20 cents; 50 copies, 40 cents; 100-400 copies, 65 cents per 100; 500 copies, $2.75.

Rental of films and filmstrips: Be sure to check with your Annual Conference Audiovisual Library to see what films and filmstrips may be available free or for nominal fee.

CREATION OUT OF CHAOS
EVALUATION SHEET

Fill out (use extra sheets if more space is needed) and mail to:

> Hilda Lee Dail
> Editor, Program Materials
> Room 1366
> 475 Riverside Drive
> New York, N.Y. 10027

1. Which programs did you use? Indicate the ones most effective.

2. Which of the additional resources listed in this book did you use?

a. Organizational handbooks:

b. Informational materials:

c. Worship resources:

d. Audiovisuals:

3. Did you follow, in general, the suggestions for presentation? _____ If not, what especially effective techniques did you use?

4. How many are in your group? _____

5. Is it a new society _____, guild _____, or circle _____? Or was this book used to supplement the regular program book _____?

6. What specific actions or projects grew out of the programs?

7. How could the book have been improved?

a. Which topics did not interest your group?

b. What additional topics should have been included?

8. Would you like to have other undated program materials? _____

CREDIT

Cover design and layout by Robert C. Houston